Praise for Megan Gail Coles a

"Are you ready for poems that pierce straight to the bone? Megan Gail Coles's *Satched* is a razor edge of fierce truth, grim humour, and unalloyed beauty. With sharp-eyed clarity and fearless candour, Coles slices open the veils of capitalism and colonization to reveal a landscape marked by poverty and resilience, violence and hope. This is Newfoundland and Labrador seen through the eyes of unconditional love and furious rage. The political, the personal, and the poetic interweave seamlessly in this debut collection, adding another genre to Coles's already impressive repertoire. *Satched* is the kind of book we need right now, the kind that confronts the real world head-on while also teaching us how to live in it."

— Kai Cheng Thom, author of *a place called No Homeland*

"Reading *Satched* is like drinking chilled wine with an old friend on a hot night, commiserating with love, gratitude, and mutual affection. It's opening a second bottle, letting the kids fall asleep watching movies, and getting out the hidden cigarettes to really get into it. It's a fist in the air before it's aimed at an appropriate eyeball. It's an exceptional accomplishment full of lyrical strength and poetic endurance."

— Katherena Vermette, author of *river woman*

"*Satched* is an acerbic, bold, and wise debut that susses out the subtle and sinister ways men infringe on women's mental and physical spaces, the horrors of the climate crisis, and the pitfalls of economic precarity. With technical mastery and an immediately infectious tone, Coles inhabits the voices of Atlantic Canada, unearths the ways grief inhabits a place, and interrogates prevailing notions of resiliency. Coles intimates both how 'our minds are poisoned against ourselves' and the ways in which kinship offers a path to forge through the audaciousness of capital and insidiousness of colonialism. Reading *Satched* is like talking to your smartest, funniest friend, who wryly declares, 'there is nothing and no one standing in your way, / except capitalism and global pandemics.'"

— Cassidy McFadzean, author of *Drolleries*

"These poems tumble into me with a rage and beauty that is oceanic. I am satched to the core. Megan Gail Coles writes poems that ask us to reconsider historical and contemporary attitudes toward poverty, race, gender, and the environment, engaging her reader in 'this present rowing over the past / to make up the future.' Because while these poems speak deeply to intergenerational trauma, solastalgia, and the systemic ills of capitalism hidden in plain sight, they are forward-looking at heart. *Satched* puts forth that despite (or perhaps because of) our human frailties, we can begin again. These poems demonstrate that repair is possible, even from a rusty scaffold, if we are willing to reach beyond ourselves."

— Clea Roberts, author of *Auguries*

Also by Megan Gail Coles

Fiction
Small Game Hunting at the Local Coward Gun Club
Eating Habits of the Chronically Lonesome

Drama
Squawk

SATCHED
POEMS

MEGAN GAIL COLES

ANANSI

Published in Canada in 2021 and the USA in 2021 by House of Anansi Press Inc.
www.houseofanansi.com

25 24 23 22 21   1 2 3 4 5

Library and Archives Canada Cataloguing in Publication

Title: Satched / Megan Gail Coles.
Names: Coles, Megan Gail, 1981– author.
Description: Poems.
Identifiers: Canadiana (print) 20210219238 | Canadiana (ebook) 20210219270 |
ISBN 9781487008949 (softcover) | ISBN 9781487008956 (EPUB)
Classification: LCC PS8605.O4479 S28 2021 | DDC C811/.6—dc23

Cover design: Alysia Shewchuk
Cover artwork (original edition): *Nine mile bog*, 2019, by Michael Pittman.
Copyright Visual Arts — CARCC, 2020
Text design and typesetting: Lucia Kim

House of Anansi Press respectfully acknowledges that the land on which we operate is the Traditional Territory of many Nations, including the Anishinabeg, the Wendat, and the Haudenosaunee. It is also the Treaty Lands of the Mississaugas of the Credit.

 Canada Council   Conseil des Arts
for the Arts   du Canada

 ONTARIO ARTS COUNCIL
CONSEIL DES ARTS DE L'ONTARIO
an Ontario government agency
un organisme du gouvernement de l'Ontario

With the participation of the Government of Canada | Canadä
Avec la participation du gouvernement du Canada

We acknowledge for their financial support of our publishing program the Canada Council for the Arts, the Ontario Arts Council, and the Government of Canada.

Printed and bound in Canada

For the young ones.
Especially Nick, Rory, and Ruby Susan.

CONTENTS

SATCHED

I HAVE BEEN A MESSY BITCH

This would be the day after;
the last of limoncello,
pulled from the corner cupboard's cobweb,
beamed brazen like a too-tight fringe
sick of giving a fuck. Knees
upon the sticky counter,
the hem of a worn nightdress
wet against the sink.
This skirting; a disgraceful parody
of limp and chinless men
not even worthy of the attention
I regret having paid them, all
erstwhile catastrophe,
required a deep throat,
a strong stomach and a scouring
to scrub clean embarrassment for having
allowed so many loathsome folk
to lick me stern to stem.

The Pinterest board
reluctantly pinned and boarded in my brain,
after years of threatening counter plots,
featured only modest wishes,
possible moderate joy
and a lot of settling.

Love-at-first-sight's storybook beginning
left out all of the ever-after parts,
leaving us woefully filling in the blanks
of good-enough-for-now
which was never good enough for anyone,
not even the b'ys.

Disappointment and frustration gave
way to morning cocktails in the kitchen.

Years before I quit smoking, I was still smoking.

And calling friends in case of emergency
which was the course, of course, taken that day,
and any day really, who the fuck are we kidding ladies,
though no real emergency emerged
to snuff out the re-emergence of my rage.

I got so many axes to grind, sparks fly,
sometimes a little hatchet hangs handy
upon the lace waistband of my panties,
confusing everyone. The men who love me
are also the men who hate me,
it was the same in grade school,
it is the same now. My metalwork
maims them, even when set on low,
it grinds all the losers I allowed inside,
and some I hadn't, that's right,
some that I had not allowed forced passage
through an unguarded doorway, the worst

sometimes
still rearing up during sleep
to gut my soft-bellied memory from within.

My reinforcements hobbled up the front steps
on crutches as I tossed bitters in a shaker, splash of lime,
a dash of kosher salt, damp from growing desperation,
to cover the sour taste on my tongue, blankets and blankets
of wicked courage got us polluted before lunch and
we yelled *fuck him* and *that other guy too* into the afternoon.

Women who drink all day never boast of drinking all day online.

Their (almost) smiling socials mimic decency or offer nothing contrary.
Do I look respectable in this one? Do I? Does she?
Side glances, sunglasses, windswept bangs, a twirl of smoke
from a cigarette held out of view.

Behind our backs is where everything happens.

Too much teeth looks suspicious, cheeky,
dishonest or drunk. Never open your mouth
or part your lips in pictures. You will
be accused of something.
Of what?
Of whatever.
Women who want to erase themselves
never take selfies with the bourbon bottle
of proof in their hand. Or joke of wine o'clock
as if the countdown ticking off miserable on their wrist

was not stalking them through the dry hours spent
worried of near-satchings in the night and what
of this or that recovery plan, just more steps to count
toward self-eradication and I hate math.
Trying to remove your mind from your body
it is not funny. Stop it, please, stop that humble
bragging, why mommy drinks
is not why women drink.

And you know it.

SOME GOOD TALKER

When the crime is finally called in
pin it on the weirdo, the bald guy,
the aging junkie in faux-torn jeans. Make it
someone's dad's fault, or what's-her-name's
uncle, say it was him, no one but he's mudder
will care, she been waiting all along
for he's ruination. Let it be this,
let him own this one for the works of us
who, having slept soundly through
the last period of game seven,
stirred straight finally
to find our team lost in triple overtime.

There were so many chances;
moments of reprieve and
near comfort
when recovery still seemed possible, it
could have gone another way had we caught
a glimpse of our own redemption,
but we missed it,
countless and irrefutable times, it sailed
by, we failed to wake and catch the tail-end of 'er,
fans of no one, our absence
sends shockwaves through the recap,
searching out answers, we yell *what happened*
and *who da fuck's in charge here*
at the Apple Box which merely plays the show.

How did we pass through such meaning making
with our eyes closed, we wonder,
but, well, truth be told, 'cause I will tell it,
we had that heavy meal,
a second serving of dessert and one too many beers,
was nearly dropping during the pregame,
reading garbage on our phones,
eyelids in dire need of clothespins long
thrown over for the machine dryer
we runs all year round
regardless of the weather.

Look here, fine day on nothing
'cept quilts on the line cause everyone likes
the look of 'em, 'specially the tourists we're meant to please.
Sin for us, tis all our fault for trusting the wrong fellow,
again and again and again we forgive without penance.
Now we owes every copper in the coffer
to buddy in the big house,
praise his name to kingdom come
and roar across the table at your wife,
while the youngsters cry into their chicken nuggets.

Some picky eaters.

The cure is also the cause.

Not enough salt on me french fries.
Can't taste nothing sure
but future gut rot and rising bile,

too tired to brush our own teeth, we collectively
lug ourselves to the bed,
forget fucking,
fucking requires facing our foul breath
and naked limbs.

The toys see, the toys in the garage are a haunting,
gets right miserable, we do, at the sight of them,
not even half paid for, yuck b'y.

Our happiness is only on loan to us,
a bribe from banks up along,
the interest set to:
unpayable.

Doomed we are, doomed from the start,
so we says fuck it then, right? Fuck no one
and everyone altogether. Fuck it!
Smoke 'em if you got 'em and we all got 'em,
laughable really, but
can't laugh no more,
joshing leads to coughing
which leads to accusations online, even
our humour hurts these days. Turns out,
oxygen is real important, too bad
we cut down half the woods
to heat rooms barely lived in,
neither footprint in the carpet floor.
The forest would be worth a fortune now,
if we'd left either stick of it standing.

Another heritage house burned last night.

Don't see how that's related, hey?

Can't face relations anywhere,
what for the pang in our chest. Needs
a pain-maker, a pace-maker, needs an upgrade on this heart
we been hard on. Life is a suffering.

Blame ignorance and public education,
the church or god. Blame the feds or local magistrates.
Blame them all.

But never blame *the companies.*
They are our true saviours. We've no
future without them. The lobbyists say so
constantly with their slick hands out for a loan. They've done
a tremendous job at changing the meaning of tremendous.
Some good talker he is. Lies like fresh cream from a young cow.

Quit it b'y. Give up believing every old foolishness on the internet.
Nothing just goes bad on its lonesome,
the economy didn't just go off like berries
along the cliff face after the first frost.
Climate change is global heating,
call it what it is or shut the fuck up about it.

Our minds are poisoned against ourselves.

Believe what you wants to believe is right.

California seethes like a low-lit pumpkin on perpetual Halloween,
the treat was the trick and we gobbled through the pillowcase stash.
This death cycle keeps death cycling without interruption,
those found guilty fall up into crown corporations
with seventy-five-thousand-dollar raises
while the pavement pulls its crumbling cover away
from the cracked curb coated in cigarette butts.
We outdid ourselves
smoking well above the national average,
truth is, get ready for it, truth is we got a bad report
exceeding in negativity, the worst is not hyperbole,
we are sometimes, in fact, the worst.

No one can say where the bodies are buried
because they are buried all over town,
in every backyard, behind
the raspberry bushes, beneath the chokecherry tree,
mind you don't let the pears linger long in the leaf fall,
their perishment will attract vermin, rats will
homestead beneath your deck feasting on
decomp in the garden, what was not hidden under
mulch and manure bought on store credit
was steamed out to sea and tossed over
to drift in the gulf current.

Unspeakable behaviours go unspoken,
but we keep thinking our thoughts, don't we?

How many criminals sit in the Tim Hortons?
The works of 'em.

Old boys shuffle decks
like priests moving parishes, while the
Oil & Gas wives living Oil & Gas lives
bark about maybe, possibly, more than likely,
having to go to work. Yes, yes, yes, yes, I knows
lots of women work but firing back
not all wives,
like not all men
or all lives matter,
misses the point of protest and unrest on purpose.

We are dying to be like each other
to be liked by each other
we are dying.

SOCIAL STUDIES

It's naive to think
any strip of this land
wasn't French before it was English,
wasn't Mi'kmaq before it was French,
Beothuk before that, though
this is a sore starting point. Genocide
is a hard fact to lay at our forebears' feet.
Yet, a primary reader taught us
our many parts banded together
to murder off innocents,
slaying inland outward,
a very convenient story for the comfortable,
who, from the safety of blame and fortune's folly,
still feel it apt and well enough
to ask at a party: why humans live
on our lonesome island anyway? Why
they ever lived there at all, really? What with
the northeasterly wind and blowing snow,
the ceaseless winter, a suffocating silence,
but for the eaves of the house deep-crooning dread
against the framework built solid and straight
from a time before we belonged to our own nation.
These awkward moments demand a swift code-shift
resulting in such knots, my lower back a knitting
of consumed ignorance, the guilt I easy absorb
enmeshed around my core as I pour
our story out over expansive kitchen tables,

gingerly saying: we live there for the same reason
anyone lives anywhere, fish washing ashore,
a glut of protein so plentiful, the isle swollen
with pride in herself, bloated with generosity that
erected you these tall buildings of which we have none
and little want for because we feel most wealthy
in the country amongst beloved company,
wood fire smoke in our damp hair, cheeks pink
from the salt and forest air, free from falsehoods
filling our frigid lungs.

ROADSIDE GARDENS

Drainage ditches shelter
our riddle fences. Squatting in peat bog
rejected by the crown, abandoned scarecrows,
now just scraps of worn cloth, wave their last threads
of bright colour, a contrast alongside every knobby
green spruce, marking it once our necessary place of living.
You can only just make out what remains
of Pop's old button-up salvaged from the ragbag
to warn off moose and caribou or some
colony of rabbits starved for cabbage heads and carrot tops,
the reddish shirt sleeve still discernible enough to cause alarm.
This backdrop of shared childhood memory
steadies us as we wind our way
toward dear kinfolk aging in their place,
holding ours together, hands right full of the arthritis,
froze through and throbbing, after all along hauling tight
the strings upon a burlap sack
where inside there waits everything.
Each passing inspires a new retelling of how it stood
upright, beforehand, as you are forever searching out words
to appease yourself, knowing that when Nan needed help
in the garden, you were too busy doing nothing and watching
nonsense, imagining the attention of boys who later
grew into men you didn't like, or hate, going to the garden
being some punishment of heritage. Labour despised
in adolescence grieves those finally grown up.
Nan and Pop having aged, no longer able-bodied enough

to dig up your favourite little tatties fresh from the autumn dirt
brought to eye level by those hands in garden gloves,
the yellow trim along the wrist: beaming.
This is a good one, look here, how many is that we got now Steve?
Then into the beef bucket, pail or bag, into the truck pan,
back to the house to rinse under the warm tap.
Go on go on a bit of dirt won't kill ya,
sure that's good for the immune system.
Skin so fine you don't even want to peel them.
All they needs, see, is a little salt,
and the smallest sliver of butter or you'll
spoil the taste, they're some good on their own
or even with a few vegetables in the pot, throw a bottle
of meat in with them and you got a stew, easy enough.
I likes a spoonful of blackcurrant jam on a slice of bread.
I takes it in to your pop while he watches the hockey,
got the TV up on blast, he have in there.
Deaf now we is see, Meggie.
And on and on and on, the sounds
of being handy to, yet held away from, what made you.

We stopped practising our culture by accident.

ONE DAY, YOU MOVE OUT

You take everything that is yours.
You take everything.

A decision decided in the dark
the night you lost faith in the grid,
safety sealed with a chair against the door
while water poured through your house.
A blessing disguised as an ice dam,
fortified by the lone slaughter
of eight mice in the kitchen, the first
met with the backside of a frying pan
swiped from atop the stove on the
morning of your dream job interview.

Knives pulled in the kitchen slice false
residual fantasies as every dress slid
along your lonesome hips hangs loose,
a slinky new number, a gift from your mother,
clings, your emancipation dress sitting slick
against your damp skin afraid of getting

caught.

Life deposited into a dining room
by a group of shabby men who confess:
moving *girls* is a lot of their business now.

You run like every weary woman before you,
a dramatic gesture never waning in drama.

Sleep in spare bedrooms, drive borrowed cars,
never find that belt you're looking for.
You pillage liquor cabinets and drink the dregs,
aloud, repeatedly, with sorrow and disgust.

You refuel yourself on children's snacks
strategically placed for grazing by a friend who
fears the cut bones appearing at sharp angles on
your face. She sleeps next to you when necessary
because you are never going back.

HOW I GOT TO THIS PLACE

I

Skipper Jack in his skiff was not the point
of my mother's story, surround-sound slapping
off the passenger seat, through the centre,
throwing her voice flat against the rear window,
to bounce back whipsaw from behind,
driving me off guard with the truth of it.

Canon Richards recounted a high-minded
rendition of sailing broadside a dory, holding a
bent man, buckled to his elbows in the salty cold cove,
only to discover with nary a shock William Williams,
Billy Williams, née William Portland, Devon-forged,
holding his country wife's tarry brow in the sea.

My mother reads French degradation like math or
science, rolling *Esquimaux* unfamiliar over her gums,
tongue protruding through a bluetooth ride,
my self-own exploitation bought near brand-new after
also coming up hot gasping and clawing from a
fixed grip, held fast 'round my body-figurative.

Skipper Jack, my mother reads, called free to
Billy, Billy my b'y, what are you doing with her?
Murderers were, and remain still, someone's b'y

even when interrupted in the act of murdering,
and Billy, best he could, responded easy enough,
I got to get rid of her sure, she's driving me crazy.

But who will feed you and wash your drawers,
says Jack to Billy who never considered womanly
drudgery and so pulls Hannah back aboard the boat,
soaked and choking on survival instincts bred down
the crack of a little tickle on our island's northern edge,
daughter to son to daughter to daughter to me.

I am the woman being drowned from the side of a dory
but I am also the man holding her shoulders under.

II

Britain wore Great Uncle Albert like a flak jacket
sent Grampy home to shriek upon the daybed
Grammy, knowing better, fussed not of what was done,
silently peeling baby potatoes from the cupboard pantry.

Grampy home from Britain shrieked upon the daybed
no one made mention of his noisy terrors but for fear
silently peeling baby potatoes from the cupboard pantry
children stock-still and horrified clenched door jambs in hallway.

No one made mention of Grampy's noisy terrors but for fear
perhaps someone should have given him a little shake or hug
children stock-still and horrified clenched door jambs in hallway
the weather fastening short pants inside the brimming saltbox.

Perhaps someone should have given Grampy a little shake or hug
dreaming of his missing brother in full view of heaving household
the weather fastening short pants inside the brimming saltbox
neither book to read clear the bible or a scatter clothes catalogue.

Dreaming of his missing brother in full view of heaving household
Grampy's kinfolk, growing longer in the limb, quietly went unnoticed
neither book to read clear the bible or a scatter clothes catalogue.
Grammy stashing the war purse away from king and country.

Grampy's kinfolk, growing longer in the limb, quietly went unnoticed
learning well and good enough affection was for weaklings
Grammy stashing the war purse away from king and country
buying up goods and services to defeat unbridled beggary.

Learning well and good enough affection was for weaklings
syllable by syllable future fathers lashed at timid feelings
still buying up goods and services to defeat unbridled poverty
Aunties swearing later over teacups Grammy was a mean bitch.

Syllable by syllable future fathers lashed at timid feelings
daughters raised for independence inside new gleaming kitchens
Aunties forever swearing over teacups Grammy was a mean bitch
having begrudged every girl child beaded candies from the counter.

Daughters raised for independence inside new gleaming kitchens
oft not bite their rogue tongues in modern conversations of old blood
having begrudged every girl child beaded candies from the counter
grateful Grammy, caring not for likeability, hauled free our forgone collar.

III

Everything north of nowhere is dry and chapped and worn,
weather-beaten eyes shadowing soft middles and harmed hearts.

Romantic extremists, such as yourself, lack the capacity to couple
though everyone is fucking or fleeing or dead inside anyway.

Your cousin hung himself in the work shed, his father shot himself atop
an old truck, another uncle in the basement while your aunt was upstairs.

From the couch your father urges you not to think on *why* as is his way
yet they built a new part on the cemetery and everyone grows cold.

Your house is the only house on the graveyard road to witness this
morbid procession, frantic, you try to warn them against complacency.

Energy escapes through the window frames so you bank snow against
low edges, heed the forecast, run home at the first puff to bar yourself in.

And the wood heat makes your nose bleed for every forest fed
the stove except when the wind is in your mouth suffocating you.

There is an aged doll laid out in your childhood crib, mourning,
sometimes you hug your mother too close, sometimes you scream.

Sure even the mean girls from high school are married with children
so you think it maybe best to not be so eager, instead, better to be mean.

Build a bony cage around your once-warm parts to meet what 'merges from
the closet, a collection of living skeletons, forever grasping at you from the dirt.

I WAS CHRISTOPHER JAMES

This was before ultrasound and Google ruined everything.
Strangers from down my father's way scanned Mom's young
belly, remarking on her small frame. Birds they are, that crowd,
built spindle-like and sharp-sheared, dark-haired and short.
Don't look like she's carrying a boy to me, neither boat builder
buried in there. And later, a girl child yanked clear with forceps,
a great bloody gash in her right dimple, soaked-on meshy
gauze in every snap. This was before plastic surgery and photoshop.
My goodness Della, look've the size of her, ten pounds, she'll wear
the biggest kind of scar on her face for always, they all dared saying. Mom
murmuring, *we should've sued that doctor, Nelson. Go on go on go on*
my dear, Dad says, *you can only just notice when she's about to laugh or cry.*
The decision decided, Megan Gail, a fine name for a stout dory, a lean skiff,
built in hard weather to take a beating, sturdy, made tough for wind and
water on her backside, strong as any boy I bet, maybe stronger still.

TIME GOES TICK TICK TICK AS TIME DOES

The wall clock that hung high in Grandmother's hallway
had a little clasp for opening the glass door,
Pop held us up to wind it with a brass key,
we took turns, it chimed, the pendulum swung,
Nanny puttered in the kitchen, buttery white toast
and milky sweet tea, all before diabetes and diet settled in.
Red the shocking colour of your hair,
much loathed as a youngster,
is now grieved after as an adult.
Womanhood is as hard as girlhood, you think,
nightly lying upon one of many beds in this family home
you bought yourself, a favoured man, who is not your boyfriend,
asks which room you sleep in, you move around a lot
because all these bedrooms are your bedrooms,
every sheet set bought brand new,
thread counts from your past, unbearable,
you do this, and more, because you are
a modern, independent woman.
This learned move beyond any train of thought
your fishing family has ever bought a ticket for
let alone boarded.
Like a criminal in the night, you sprint alongside,
toss your luggage in, a dog, fuck it,
another dog, you get whatever you want,
you work hard. There are times when there are tears,
when you are tired, willing someone else to change the blown bulb,
its fixture well out of reach, you get nervous upon a dining room chair

dragged along reluctantly before quitting again
to retire to the couch, horizontal like, where's that flicker gone.
But there is also much merry, glasses of champagne,
friendships like summer sunshine on your face and
in your stead, behind your back, long after all your sails are set,
you hope they say she was brave and kind in a time
when bravery and kindness were not in fashion
and those who loved her, loved her well and always for it,
because she was so truly just herself
no matter the trends trending
or coming hardships.

HERE COMES YOUR LATE THIRTIES

You start closing doors
downstairs to fix in
the heat up top
rising and drawing
through cracks you
forever fail to fill
half a mind to
plastic-parcel-wrap
yourself inside this house.

Late fall birthdays mean
the sun arrives just in time
to set as the cold rolls in.

Pull on another sweater
you could never afford
to parade around bare-
assed anyway.

Search out last winter's
wool that went into
storage unwashed,
a faint whiff of hope
off the once-already
darned sock heels.

Every day is death
and dusk
and eating salad alone.

You tell your mother,
long distance,
that you will wear your
blue lace dress
to a younger cousin's wedding.
Some days later she buys
the same lace dress in black
because your mother delights
in being mistaken for her own child.

Every year you were aged up beyond yourself.

You learned to fry pork chops
on the stovetop at nine
while your dad slept
on a rose-coloured couch in the next room.
"Latch key" would suggest a latch
but no one locks their doors
having always so much family
about the place appearing
to rear collectively while
the pig fat sprung and popped
at your naked hands.

Every frying pan
is lodged atop some fire

just waiting and you girl
are a jumper.
Throw yourself a party and worry
no one will come like a sad
adolescent unsure of her
standing in a small circle,
confidence hard-etched,
chipped
and scraped clear,
sharp rock on flat rock,
your determination sometimes
leads to heavy drinking atop
the kitchen counter as
the room surges brimful
to bursting with affection.

Every news outlet proclaims there
are black panthers here now
and women well-versed
in the realities of daily living near
large prey animals
snicker at the fellows wallowing
online for their newly
infringed-upon freedoms.

You bribe the dogs in
from the fenced yard
for fear of another
bad thing happening.

Every cake has more candles
even though you're so nearly
winded and there is no one
handy to lean in and help
blow out the blaze.

"150% CHANCE OF COMMITTING ANOTHER CRIME"

A serial offender with 97 charges on his ticker tape
darts back inside where the mental-health doctors
have already suspended him from intense sex rehab.
He's a challenging participant, a poor candidate, town
can look forward to him again in 445 days with time
and a half credited for time served after hiding in a
duck blind, pants down, exposing himself to women
along the trail. Has a history of harming and killing
small animals, been diagnosed with concurrent illnesses,
a high-risk sexual predator with violent tendencies
who likes to keep pace around the university even
though he was ordered to stay clear of campus. Previous
incidents include holding a gun once to a family
member's head, threatening to push another relation
down over the stairs, says himself there is 150% chance
he will reoffend. Carried a knife into a dance studio attached
to a daycare, pressed his penis into a window facing
a collection of teenage girls, their dance instructor took
a video screaming for him to leave, though he returned later,
cock in one hand, blade in the other. On the registry for life,
banned from all parks, swimming holes, playgrounds, schools,
any location locating kids whom he admits to searching out.
Has no insight into his behaviour but flips his middle finger
to the judge in court and pulls his sweater over his head to
conceal against the media. Obviously some psychological
issues need addressing everyone agrees, though no
one acknowledges there is nowhere to address them.

So the man is turned back out into the public, having
proven his unavoidable intention over the whole of his
lifetime, to wild roam terrorizing the city and himself
until he rapes and murders a woman or a child if he has
not done so already. What do we know, how could we know?

GOOD MORNING SUN

You wake at first light, summer damp and birdsong flung in through cracked windows, crows provoking robins on the line, seagulls scream in the cookie factory parking lot, across your brow there is sweat, you are already thinking insolvency thoughts, you dream of murderers, of your mouth calling out and making no noise, what happened to your voice, did you ever find it, your phone, your phone, your phone was next to the pillow, and the dogs, they never bark in your nightmares, where are the dogs, their quiet, at first horrifying, becomes a steady reassurance, your dogs bark, this is how your safe space was furnished, a man taught the brown dog not to, but that man did not love you, thankfully the black dog knows nothing of anything and barks at liberty, cars, the post, other dogs many streets over, a neighbourhood away, both dogs now together joyful, diligent barkers, someone is coming, someone is here, someone, but this bark-less morning yanks you from rest, elsewhere there is hygge, here there is only hag, you nightly apply a cold cream called wedding mask to ward off worry, the irony of it makes you cry more wrinkles into your face, you will yourself back to sleep, eight hours is necessary to stay alive, that's what the books say, all the books you read so you don't die, but there's nothing to it, you only sleep in when you drink out and the books say that doesn't count, you wonder if you've ever slept correct, there was a week in January you thought things might be nice, but that is the past, now you are crystalline, your bladder hates your guts, it is all a mess of rivalry in the middle, you pee the rushing pee of impending kidney failure before throwing hard coffee atop the works, it is necessary to daily shock yourself into your life, a violent jolt is required to activate some urgency, otherwise it is just numbness, a blank stare, the screens, you will have to get on Tinder to prevent from sleeping with your ex, it seems more than likely you were deprived contact in infancy, by nine o'clock you need a nap, caffeine does not shift easily, sighs escape the body, you want the Indigenous, Black and

Brown girls to win everything but you also want to win something, it seems you cannot all be comforted at once, you are carved clear separate of them, on your own, a military of one, the vagina army was disbanded, you were not aware of the disbanding, you just were suddenly on the field staring at bleachers void of a cheering section, it was a gradual depletion, everyone loves the mystery, no one loves the truth, and more than anything you wish you had felt pretty when you were pretty, people told you so while you survived on counted cashews and desperation, your bank account hints you will be beautiful again soon enough, everything everywhere is named after rich people, the only thing called for you is your growing saga of pain, the silence of people not caring is deafening, crickets would cricket but it is too cold for all that noise, there is nothing but motorbikes in the night, a few domestics and sirens wailing until the birds start a racket on the line again and you reach out to stroke the dogs.

LAY YOUR WHISPER ON SOME OTHER PILLOW

Please, yes,
do mansplain it to me,
the answer I've searched
my whole life to find just
happens to be in your pants,
had I known I would not
have wasted the time —
hours, minutes, seconds —
all units of measure,
trying to solve the problem you
can deduce and pardon
in a mere sentence or two,
your genius thesis slow-boiled
to a steady simmer
so my pea-sized brain
can absorb fully
the sheer brilliance
biology doled out
to you alongside that
cock you hope is huge
and you there
in shock now
that I only ever wanted you
to listen when I have been
this whole time doing all
the hard
and heavy lifting,

well, honestly,
I was very tired or
just wanted to undress,
surprise, surprise, arsehole,
you don't have the market on sex
cornered like you thought,
so talk dirty to me or
shut the fuck up.

APPOINTMENT NOTIFICATION

All your friends are broke and overworked and anxious.
Everyone pays a stranger to listen to them weep.
You throw a box of tissues at your counsellor
on a sunny Saturday afternoon when
you would rather be swimming or hiking.
You wonder aloud if you're a bad person,
piling snotty wads of Kleenex upon a little table.
Your tossing frustration nearly spills a glass of water:
this desperate tipping point scares even you
so you apologize for fear of being rejected
by a woman employed to monitor your stress.
She advises you not to do anything
that will make matters worse
but you don't make promises you can't keep anymore.
That road is well trod upon and you are trying for…honesty?
Or some half-respectable proximity to acceptance.
Everyone and their kid is practising mindfulness
which is funny as you are so mindful your jaw hurts.
You worry your hair will fall out from concentration,
every follicle sears as if scraped by a dull razor of focus.
You are the blunt blade rubbing yourself raw.
The single man who texts you on a Friday night
is an ex who only loves you when you don't love him.
You wonder if you are a flat line in a sea of swirls
as you call about rental insurance and damage deposits.
The men you have cared for would not get their money back,
what with the stingy regard you were brazenly paid, but

no funds exchanged hands as you have long thought yourself
worthless and undeserving of investment monetary or otherwise.
What's the point, why bother, who cares, we're all gonna die.
If it were just you who felt like this maybe you'd stand a chance but
all your friends are broke and overworked and anxious.

DESPERATION BOOKS THE FERRY

You read genius-food books hoping your old brain will brain better,
as your imposter syndrome flashes forward, confidence in fast retreat
Force-feed yourself tablespoons of extra virgin olive oil near the sink
the little charge when you swallow suggests a scorching
Hoping this small sizzle indicates a synapse fire overhead
The kind of kindling that results in stronger carbon
You'll need to outfit yourself in a shiny new battle kit now
Sure this whole undertaking has been undertook before
A decade ago you rode the same ferry in the return direction
How old will you have to be before you are an adult woman
You cast off drinking alcohol and vow to never dance again
Nearly immediately you shake cocktails and put on a record
What of poverty what of property tax what of education
You can't afford to do it but you can't afford to not do it
There is nothing and no way of affording anything at all for you
Your boat came in and set sail again in barely a puff of wind
You missed it while off bawling over some man who didn't love you
You want to argue there never was a jesus boat for you to safely board
You were never meant to get this far anyway you are some lucky girl
some lucky.

BROKEN EMOTIONAL MANAGER

Your emotional manager is broken,
it did not work properly from go,
too much pressure was placed on
its untested system, not nearly enough
supervision was provided, there was
little to no orientation before your
promotion to emotionally manage
the trajectory of the brand-new
managers added to the network.
More is not merrier as the saying goes,
it is in fact further taxing every laden
emotional manager handy by proxy,
constantly buffering a slow drain
without a plunger or plumber whose
emotional manager never worked
at all either, it was always a patch job,
barely holding this outfit together,
don't look in the cupboards
or the linen closet, you will find
it all ways flung in, heaving
behind the barely held-closed
door, so much tension on the latch,
everyone aware one day there will
come a crash when the neglected
emotional manager is overwhelmed
entirely by the loaded scheme. All
humans about the place claiming

shock and disdain when the bow breaks,
the streets now a flood of damaged
feelings that we all knew were throbbing
other side the dam, pretend pretend
all you wants that it comes as some surprise
but we've all been seated at that dinner table
thinking, over tea, that something is
wrong with this one or that one
and all of us, though, these thoughts, went nowhere
until the breaking point broke your emotional
manager who deserved so much better.

THE TRADES

Once upon a July you synced your breakdown
with the washer exploding soapy water onto
the unfinished laundry room floor while your face
leaked relentless during the summer heatwave.

The wet cement and lumber refused to re-dry
in the damp basement where the cat peed and
the walls were not painted enough or at all behind
the couch strategically placed for obscuring flaws.

Your elder puss began to daily relieve himself
beyond the boundaries of his piss box because
the mould in the basement was a confusion to him
and you alike but there was no one to ask or help.

You'd no boyfriend as a learned safety precaution
and your father was sick and tired of being your
father having ages ago built in bookshelves and
mended ceilings over another man's enjoyment.

You search the lady network for a trustworthy
man that might put your pipes in order once
and for all with the weary wisdom aware of the
pink tax taxing limited income and patience.

A man you know says he is a contractor this
information loosely confirmed acts as insurance

to push through fog and feline scent of routine
hatred seeping from beneath the laundry door.

The contractor says he needs to start right away
your basement renovation will take just three
weeks and he is doing you a huge favour which
you accept as truth because you kind of know him.

This is your first mistake that and giving him your
house-key which he claimed will make everything
easier and you never thought to ask because you
don't know you're even allowed to ask *easier for who?*

A parade of the contractor's guys start invading
your house where you work there's a stereo directly
under your desk blasting out pop music and classic
rock while everyone asks to speak to your husband.

Five weeks into the three-week reno you go to Ireland
to celebrate still being alive with your best friend who
is celebrating the same there are no walls when you
leave and there are no walls when you return.

The book you are writing is not getting written
you hemorrhage money into the basement frame
new guys you know only as actors and bartenders
are qualified to carpenter because they are men.

All the quotes you were quoted are incorrect but
you can pay them under the table another favour

you are meant to be grateful for though you've little
recourse now they've hauled the radiators off the wall.

The electrician's guy whom he has never had a problem
with leaves cigarettes burning in his truck's ashtray and
just walks away the smoke trails from the cab into your
window you can see the keys in the ignition the cherry.

He wants to know how you can afford this asks repeatedly
how much you paid for your house daily implying that
if you can afford your independence and that new car
in the driveway then you can afford to pay him whatever.

Another day you arrive home to find the door wide
open on your empty house housing your meagre
worldly goods and your dogs who would never
navigate a city street if accidentally found upon them.

You sit and weep on the retaining wall because you
have once again trusted the wrong man to keep your
homestead safe and the new bathroom does not work
and you live in the red for years constantly fearing collections.

YOU COULD HAVE SAID NO

You've only slept with two wrong men
in as many years but still consider yourself a slut.
When the young doctor smiles and gently asks
if you're symptomatic, you shake your shameful head,
tell her no, just stupid and scared you want to say,
want to tell her how the last resident winced
after having shoved the much-too-large metal speculum
up your sorry pussy, you all the while whimpering,
I've never given birth, never birthed a baby,
have issues with anxiety, you want to tell her
how the resident wanted to keep trying, to get it right,
your damp ass lurching off the paper, clutching hold,
tight-clamped, nearly passing out, cold and unconscious,
confessing you are a fainter with a low physical pain threshold,
which is a trying irony given your emotional rigour,
you want to tell her how your blood pressure crested the danger wave
as the resident practised, inserting and reinserting, pushing past
your weak-willed concerns as you softly begged the doctor
to intervene, half-puffed syllables attempting to revoke some
permission never truly requested, your womanhood assumed accessible,
the contempt wafting at you for ruining this opportunity at studious perfection
before you lie alone, whipped, in a windowless room, sweating
from your every pit, weeping, because you should have said no
to being taught upon, yet again, like some pin-cushion, crash-test dummy,
triggered half to death over here but you can't even form a no at home,
let alone in a hospital where all the coats are bleached brighter than your clear collar
which shows its denim base and break-line each time you are acted upon.

RUN BITCH RUN

Get yourself a fuck boy
while your body holds
while the snow falls
while your phone's lit
while you've propane in the tank.

Get yourself a fuck boy
before your cat ages out of the pen
while that feline-driven part still retains
enough hunger to wash her hair.

Five minutes ago
you were too young
and now you are too old
the middle place where
you are just right

does not exist.

INSIDE MY HEAD THERE ARE RUMOURS

I am sorry to all the women I have hated for the wrong reasons
And to the men I have not adequately loathed for all the right ones
Here we call colonialism Canada elsewhere they call it Australia or Brazil
CIBC owns my house my car my debt and the first-born child I'll not have
Father says I'll never get a man if I don't learn how to relax so I rage at him
All these family photos full of ex boyfriends are ruined now sure ruined
Can't gut fish bead earrings step dance or play the accordion
The only thing I'm good at fetches few dollars and even less respect
Nan says I never calls her back when she calls me which is lies for her
I forgot my grandfather's birthday because I inherited his depression
All I wants is for everyone to fuck off already (and a ride out in boat)
You wouldn't know but mainlanders never get drunk in summer
Mom thinks picking fights with her daughters is demonstrating love
The poodles missed their grooming appointment and I feel guilty
Yet again the sink is not draining at optimal sink-draining speed
If the plumber doesn't re-plumb the bathroom I'm gonna start a row online
I went to a meeting expecting to be evicted and left chair of the board
I loves it when tourists teach me about my homeland like I am a daft punk
We fast feed golden food to our cancers and complain about health care costs
Got the largest Costco in all the country (and fastest-rising unemployment)
My overdue time which never came took a very longer time never coming
Dogs are the best investment I ever made in my own longevity
My nephew makes living suck less with every new word he says aloud
I French braid Z's hair because it makes Maria happy (and prevents head lice)
I refuse to Like your Facebook photos when we all know your husband's a dick
Date rape is like poverty I just accept it as inevitable and brace myself
I have watched everything good on Netflix which is not fit to talk about

They announce breaking ground on the new hospital ten years running
Romanticize my childhood trauma for your gain and watch me come aboard you
I'm never going to meet the love of my life in my best friend's living room
Reading my thoughts on paper is not as hard as having them.

MADE RIGHT HERE (OR NOT)

You can get Screeched-in somewhere near Bloor and Spadina now
Become an honorary Newfoundlander while on vacation in New York
You needn't even lower yourself onto berry bog to spoil in the exploits
The Broadway crowd paid for a tourism ad and Gander rejoiced
Never mind the commercial slaughter of your long-mocked tongue

But for one beloved member we've got hardly a pony in that stable
Let alone the race if we were another community we'd cry token
Instead the Government lauds art made manifest on the mainland
This great celebration of clear exploitation rings out eternal!

If they are stealing from us it proves we are actually here, right?

Each song clip passively consumed on social media hurts your bones
Apparently there is nothing about us that is not for sale at lousy prices
Neighbours criss-cross the pond to take in the London production
The whole trip put on credit as the paint peels from the clapboard
Meanwhile all and sundry begrudge the local band five dollars on the door

But the cast wished you Happy Canada Day on Facebook so you know

This means more than some starving artist alongside crafting poems
She never writes of anything jolly anyway no one's knighted in her prose
A mentor informs you without irony that a Newfoundlander could not write it
You beseech him access and ownership and trauma but your voice goes unheard

Everyone points to economic envy like it was not wholly proving your tired point
No Newfoundlander could ever write the most famous Newfoundland play

Our story belongs to some other smarter better person come from away.

YOU CANNOT ALWAYS BE BEAUTIFUL

Sometimes you are under-slept
sweat-stained sporting yesterday's
eye lines heavy upon weary cheeks
backaches and bloat having eaten
not enough of anything good and
too much of all available evil
sugar and bubbles
dubious thoughts of grandeur
mix with lingering self-doubt
you wave off with jokes though
you find little of anything very funny
unfocused rambling fears
as you attempt connection
knowing one misstep
will see you strung up
strange nights deliver you
to empty rooms where you
confess to your beloved via text
there is never sufficient water in the body
daily forgetting the persistent drought
only to pour more in fast-flood fashion
overwhelming the small store of space
which is only human because you are only human
unfit to sustain yourself in any routine
satching your own pot
an overwatered houseplant

unwilling to flower
as our nature tends toward
moments of too much
when all we have is not enough.

ONE SATURDAY MORNING

Hard-palate bridge-work
supports plastic wired-in class reminders
of shame and fear. Never are we more full of fright
than reclining in a dentist chair, having hardly vocabulary
or insurance to protect or parental guidance to prevent.
Only bright boxes of sugary love marketed between
moments of our captured attention, a flood of colour,
cartoons we absorbed absently cross-legged on the floor
slurping up the last sloppy dregs with sweet ease,
before tipping our bowls level to, but below,
eye-line so as not to obscure the message.
Programming is the right word for it.
Every day educated to mindlessly gobble until the canine spaces
came clear off, premolars dropping wild from maxillas,
first snowflakes on the edge of storms,
beautifully undervalued like Nan's knit mittens,
our mandibles signalling the loss,
held-fast roots clasping our ossein strength
incrementally damaged
during requests for forgiveness,
in times of struggle,
because there was no way to give what was necessary.
Our ancestral confidence rotted away before any
myelin came in to insulate these tired nerves
from every day being
marginally scared to death of dying,
as the very pulp of a person falls atop frightened tongues,

taking the wind right out of the body. A fought tiger
loses its tooth before slowly
lumbering off to die.
You gave us all you had been given which
was so much less than you deserved.

FOOD THESE DAYS

Pink ribbon yogurt in single-use plastic pods
harbour convenient brews for growing tumours in your breast.
A witchy potion feeding carcinogens to baby through milk
once made perfect having evolved naturally in the body,
since interfered with by military scientists and profiteers.
Knock knock! Who's there? A free market?
The dogs didn't even rouse an alarm. Evil comes
collecting, unannounced, coiled and clawing
your wounded confidence as guilt and cowardice
strangles all: fins, furs, fingers and feathers.
We run rampage along the riverbank.
Forget ourselves and ignore our burning guts,
such suffocating flames. I'm unable to pull
a swallow of air inside. Listen here,
breathing is more important than cheese!
Yet the children cannot run without a puffer.
Who made that hard blue elbow?
So much mucus sits atop the lungs, the sticky state of us.
We look away from the slaughter to start emergency funds
funding allowable pus, waging war on the living.
Little legs unable to stretch beyond a confined space, tis nothing
but modern evil to shelter such violence due to notions of sameness.
Conform, they said! Be like Mike,
or Fred, or John, be like man,
be manly, consume with little regard.
Feel no feelings. How is any of all of this pain permitted?
How does it travel into our futures? Seven generations,

eight, nine, we stopped counting ages ago.
Maybe it is cultural. Or maybe it is capitalism.
They've made a pill for everything except what ails us.
You piss some new illness into the water well
and feel like dying, *we* all get cancer
if we live long enough. But *we all* don't.
Who doesn't? Ask yourself who doesn't. And why?

PUBLIC SWIMMING POOLS

Your counsellor prescribes pre-emptive swims
so you search out public swimming pools all over the country
for fear of relapse as the fall crests an overwhelming wave of uncertainty.
You irritate half of everyone in bright rooms with demands for equality
because you can't *just be grateful* for the space they made at their table,
temporarily allowing you a moment at the mic, covering your
room service, a garden salad with grilled salmon and a smoothie
costs eighty-five dollars. You imagine telling your nan this later
before deciding you best not soak her so thoroughly
with more proof of the world's easy disdain.
Instead, you send her selfies from every city, all these green rooms,
you kitted out in your red dress, that blue blazer, trying,
desperately, to be taken seriously.
Your nan prefers pictures with your new boyfriend outside.

You know this because she tells you, repeatedly,
asking when he will come meet her, claiming she will be dead soon,
not gonna make it to another wedding, she goads, though
she's no illness beyond her chronic inheritance and number of her age.
Your brain surfs its way toward her coast through these pool-lit lanes,
soft pop music playing, some teenager seated overtop you,
a bored expression upon her lips, your lean lover butterflying alongside
knows not of where your mind travels until later in the car when you share
stories of the change room, him having out of character made small talk
with a stranger, claiming this is to your credit, his happy shift toward generosity
is a happy shift. You trade back your recounting of a woman, maybe your age,
maybe older, hardened with the heft of living, proof worn 'round her waist,

a grave tire she is forced to lug after bearing her many children,
only the one boy sporting hair of any natural colour, his siblings streaked through.
The tween suddenly whipping antisemitism at her littlest little sister
knows nothing of Judaism, knowing only the power of adult words,
hatred slung the room's length in syllables, the shock on your face caught
by a mother quick to recognize you take offence, the steady swallow,
a humbling navigation, this woman scolding her pink and purple haired daughters,
barking to *shut their mouths or she'll shut it for them*, saying this clearly
for the benefit of your ears and you take in the worn swimwear,
the handful of youngsters, no one to help her herd them at this early hour,
where she is trying to teach all to swim or enjoy their childhood.
The tween tossing racism so freely, you nearly swing 'round at these people,
having nothing to defend the empty change room from but ignorance,
heaving it at each other like a towel flicked in jest
though your hidden beginning stops any offering further shame.

You want these children to have the nice pool as you
sometimes had the nice pool when you needed a place.
They cannot even comprehend the disgrace showered upon them
in public spaces for appearing so poorly as to not know
the meaning of words in their mouths in the context of the world
because the world is so far beyond these children and their mother
who wants you to know they have been swimming before,
going well out of her way to loudly share this information
which sounds like a small plea for patience and a threat,
do not embarrass me now here in front of my children,
she cannot know you lived in a trailer once too,
had your phone regularly unhooked,
ate no name cheese slices after school every day,
saltines and toast keeping you alive through junior high,

how you won't go handy to Kraft Dinner having sworn
KD can fuck off now and forever but remembering well
powdered cheese, knowing you knew nothing, reliving that feeling again
and again and again, travelling two weeks at a time to another town
for swimming badges, a whole community deciding en masse
no more children would drown in the lake, pond or brook, over
the wharf, the side of a dory, no more, enough, driving
through snowstorms and moose-covered roads only to arrive
in slightly larger places where our parents were constantly
found wanting, ignorant and vulgar, because they too
were taught to speak hate casually as children, the slow re-education
that ensued when you discovered, in your twenties, all the bad things
you did not know you said, all the once informing your whole clan
of mistaken harm, can't say that, or that, can't say that either,
half your words were wrong words stinging slaps upon a cheek.

So no, you couldn't or wouldn't or won't taint the pool for those kids
who are judged enough already for how and where they were born,
instead you hope that learning to swim will bring sufficient
strength to pull themselves, stroke after stroke, lap after lap,
up and out of this crude shallow water of disregard.

CHRISTMAS TRUCE THE ONCE I SUPPOSE

It's row upon row of the people you know echoing
as you silent-sway in the rear stairway beyond view
atop deep-red carpeting befitting a united church
surrounding walls draped in thick layers of pale pink
the polished banister winding all ways out of reach
face upturned to the ceiling arms stretched above
yourself matching pale-pink knitwear a gesture of
uneasy joy this feeling with your finger in the pages
holding your place ready to greet them with kindness
pleasure rarely felt is unrecognizable and nothing like
your usual rage you try to name the difference inside
the space where dread held residence beforehand
when any holiday triggered loss and humiliation
raising voices from the past ghosts recalling your
disappointment and distrust in days dictating pure
feelings as if the calendar can decide men's hearts
now each night your cousin's band plays you in
to read the gentlest pieces of your rural story to this
urban brethren always fearful of the wild words hot
off tongues of bay relations who have taken the brunt
of hardship these hundreds of years now forming new
sentences so unpredictable in temperament the city
sits up awestruck having never known the capacity
beyond the overpass was so boldly ambitious the
stage a supporting cast of one-time bay kids now
grown-ups singing sad sweet and sickly melodies
soothing honesty ringing blessed through the nave

you joining the call for collectivity refusing all hateful
division as you caution patience for the homeless men
at the locked front door having chosen to pound
their menace upon the church steps wearing Santa masks
so sinister and apt broadside this lukewarm ginger display of
friendship, a truce as you their stormy northern daughter
poke them for their follies and they feel seen and understood
a part of your good fortune which they are so you pay them
great heaping servings of gratitude and pride but warn
you will swear at them another day that is not this concert as
they sly-smile understanding at your determination to be heard.

LIFE IN THE FIRE LANE

A white double cab is parked in the fire lane
at the island's triumphant Costco on a slushy
Saturday afternoon where shoppers of every
shade and background are slow-blended in the
bread-mix of shared cultural hegemony now
all the little family shops have foreclosed their
doors due to a pinch of poverty and a lavish
spoonful of spite inherited from times before
this time when one crowd attempted to pull
up above every other crowd in the cove and
fuck them for their difference hates them for
their lack of modesty look of 'em now thinks
some lot of themselves is just an oppressive way
of describing confidence which was not handed
out equally to many of us in this checkout line
with a cart full of plastic we would never buy in
our bays because all things bought in our bays
are lesser things by default we'd sooner drive
hours over snow-covered roads a near-miss with
the wood truck the fright of your life until the next
time you runs out of toilet paper which must be
bought in conflict-sized quantities in one man's
legacy placed many kilometres from your bathroom
and by the thundering jesus everyone says they
need when they really mean they *want* having
accidentally forgotten the distinction of words ages
ago when TVs were first turned on in living rooms

across the land and then in bedrooms and then in
dining rooms and then in every room in the house
some in the shed background noise to sleep under
we've no need to talk at all now even though we've
want, wait, need, wait, but our unused tongues lay
decades dormant in our frustrated mouths and now
we've no language left to describe the urgency we
feel over getting home before dark an anxiety of living
held in the body the works of us behaving with little love
or dignity like this woman loading the white double-cab
pan full up of purchases in the freezing rain her elderly
father alongside her cowering no gloves on cars barc
a shiver running through them as she there full of rage
bawls her life's frustrations at the minimum wage cart
collector when he informs about the fire lane and safety
just doing his job hands holding the line of cold wet
shopping carts before him between them and she sees
her fear of being poor and looking poorly and so
fury flings aggression at the only person handy to her
she can reach and it goes on and on and perhaps we should
have intervened on his behalf but we too were just trying
to get home to our brothers and best friends warm light
and soft pants something strong in our cups under a wool
blanket so we might whisper plan our own attempt at a little joy.

NEPHEW

I

Tommy at the intersection of Mont Royal and Papineau
looks nothing like your nephew but every Inuk man feels
a part of his story which is now part of your story too blended
together your northern family is all ice pans and seal pelts
wood fires fish netting never ceasing unease and love.

When Tommy bounds into traffic with his paper cup your
heart leaps large in your throat as you watch him from the
cold curb worried his bright eyes will be quick-dimmed by
someone's unearned fear and disdain which is so plentiful
it makes you want to scream and cry and fight to the death.

Later Tommy again roughhousing with a buddy on the
icy sidewalk laughing and carrying on like life cannot harm
the shielded parts within him he is a sprinter an agile darter
of metro ledges weaving on the escalator his companions call
wait bellowing him back as we sink further into the city bowels.

Another day Tommy is speaking Inuktitut with a woman you
have heard loudly arguing with a white man on the street and
you wonder after your nephew's acquisition and promise you
will learn at least as many polite words as you would on holiday
in a foreign land that was not his or yours or ours together.

Ajak means aunt who is a mother's sister and you are one of
many trying to comb your way over cobble beaches beneath

tried tuckamore fitfully formed upon snarled breastplates a legion of broken hands worn across centuries of roughly made decisions benefiting only those holding the correct words in their mouths.

Tommy hangs around the front door of the neighbourhood Dollarama talking to the man who camps cross-legged on the cement lip near the light post and you wonder what his aunties wished for him as a child what they wish for him still and your big sister wants all racism abolished before any sting can settle.

II

Two Newfoundland men are banned from our provincial
skies for every ounce of bad behaviour on display well into
their cups on the milk run home from Labrador which has
provided them bread and butter regardless of their ignorance
and this vicious colonialism is a plague on all our houses.

The men don't even know Eskimo is not a funny joke to heave
at elders seeking treatment on the island they don't even know
it is gross to pseudo-hump the stewardess behind her back or
that ancient languages sound odd only to unaccustomed ears
all they know is a livelihood is lost to them in this exchange.

The company that exploits us all has used them to make
an example of supposed intolerance while the corporate
beast we bow down to en masse determines the rough passage
of all living things water animals dignity and time of which we
have none each thin caribou ticking off the decline on our watch.

And while you know the men's disrespect is not solely their own
but the perfect product meant to separate us from each other your
urgent heart wants all thoughtless vulgar men confined to the earth
forever where they're unable to skyward haul down your nephew's
idea of himself and ground it to dirt with their callow casual hate.

Your kinship is his kinship now an allegiance well suited his new-
found crowd dogged half-feral ones besot and devoted to ideals
of fairness and learning and b'ys oh b'ys we got to do better now
the future depends on our children navigating these cruel paths
we swamp through this ages-mangled and rotten undergrowth.

MOLE SISTER AND OVER BEAR

Mole Sister retreats to her borrowed burrow
three days running as Over Bear attempts to
quiet herself with reminders of depressions past
to prevent a snarling impatient emergence
from a self-enforced hibernation knowing only
after years of scratching and clawing at found
foul birchbark in the hopes of nourishment that
it serves no one to wake the seasonally affected to
an uproarious uprising in the name of sisterhood and
better living this being impossible to fathom no
inkling of light beyond this ceaseless darkness
with the only gleam glimmering off Over Bear's
yellowing teeth fully revealed in frustration and
guilt having not raised Mole Sister right as a cub
feelings a well of regret inside faulty family caverns
housing generations of inexperienced whelpers
Mole Sister while acknowledging Over Bear's
ignorance and youth cannot help but hold all
accountable for her inability to hovel out a hearth
and so she sinks further beyond body cleanliness
refusing foodstuffs meant to fulfill rejecting soft
intentioned care fading into the ancient fledgling
deprivation that delivered her coltish Over Bear
to the position of primary child-rearer having not
two digits of earthly training on how to nuzzle any
kind of Mole Sister out of solitary notions of self
and this lonesome artery beneath bright surfaces
needs cutting and capping from the original source

of inheritance though our native bearing lacks
the ability to counter hundreds of years of shrinking
into the depths of birthing with surviving alone being
the only goal as if staying alive were the same as
living and Over Bear looms large in demeanour
having found the only escape route from buried
burrow is unrelenting digging so goes the silent
gouging angry hoeing so goes the smooth hand-off
of low-minded unfurling transferring flaws warm with
childish devotion between Over Bear and Mole Sister.

RACING MACHINES

Polar bear paws pad messages into a kitchen bridge
five coves from your cove, visible through patio doors,
clear deliberation of a hungry traveller parading circles
'round a lit entrance, shared across all social platforms on
Boxing Day, the Straits humming with the premature arrival
of our annual visitor who should be hunting north of here
many more months than this. Like a startled host, hands filthy
and fully unprepared, we're put out by our early guests, we
gripe over our shock endlessly in porches, storm doors
held ajar behind us in case we must necessary speedy flee
from open-concept houses warmed to boiling by another
section of forest fed the fire, ambling around in our naked
feet, summer-polished toenails year-round now, paying
no heed to the winter calendar, fuck nature, fuck da cold,
I hates socks, hates 'em, Grandmother pounds around
her table making space for more protein and fat, *have a
bit of apricot cake*, Nanny's favourite, love in a bread pan,
*when we were girls you could go over to Labrador in
the komatik*, travel the coast atop the pack ice, bundled
in the sleigh box. But the harbour never freezes now,
ponds no longer safe for crossing, a cousin's boyfriend
crashed into frozen slob ice blown up from the thawed
lake amidst a January gale, a hard rivet placed in his
path, brought up solid, he was thrown, and died, in the
middle of a Saturday night that should have been nice
riding. Nothing we grew to know is what it is anymore,
all of everything shifts underfoot, these new conditions

are not our lived conditions, we must relearn the land again,
what's the weather doing out there, she's raging b'y, angry
old day on the water on the land on the road angry old day.
Your uncle and the volunteer fire brigade brought your
cousin's man in from the country, everyone does what they can,
though they'll never unsee the likes of it, never unknow this raw mar,
how much sorrow can our little place hold, this much, this much, more?
Our father stops at the lake edge to kick fresh powder on the track,
racing machines are not built for slow going over the wood paths,
they overheat from confinement, got to open up the throttle on
the flats or even the best machine will run hot and be spoiled.

GOOD NIGHT MOON

Put yourself down like a hurt child
having flailed against bedtime
these last quick years,
tormenting all sensible people handy:
the full length of the hall,
up the stairs, in protest,
your once-fiendish grousing gripped the railing,
a little foot, struck out in frustration,
cracked itself off the banister,
memories of a broken toe
throb in your shoe some evenings
after a run or a bit of rain
this was you, see,
you were like some reluctant wild writhing thing,
having lost all sense of routine,
tired and sober again,
you discovered you forgot all correct ways
of sound sleeping, consumption is up
but the body is a hollow sad sack,
rigid nerves smack against a brick wall of worry
that sits to the right of your gut, knotted and aggrieved,
everything disturbs you,
sleep debt, like all debt, is accumulating,
your generation rouses itself, looks over its shoulder,
finds it's napping broadside the poorhouse,
we spent lavishly, or what little we had,
on the wrong people at the worst time,

a decade of bad investment,
we called it our twenties,
this costly lot cost a lot,
and everyone is reading up on the basics,
sourdough starter kits and dental floss, a lot of stretching,
remember falling asleep without fear of not falling asleep,
without strategy, deliberate preparation,
YouTube videos about nature, that blue screen growling in your face
every connective device is self-sabotage,
but so is loneliness, now we know,
autoplay is worse than smoking a pack a day,
old you had been known to just
roll with it, go with it,
call fuck it to get on with it, text it into the night,
are you still watching, am I? Of course, we are!
Stupid questions abound, ignorance and addictions galore,
who can turn away from this shit-show, right?
Anything could happen sure these days
and it will,
just give it a minute
and a decent wifi connection,
the world will keep you up, ask Nan, wild-eyed,
she sleeps in the morning having kept her vigil all night
cause half of humans in charge are sociopaths,
the others: magnificently greedy
and/or oblivious,
inside the overlap there
are just ordinary murderers and rapists,
the business community, you know, men,
making appointments and decisions,

promoting policies for the pillage
while the help rears the youngsters
on usurped privileges and stolen money, land, rights, indeed,
you dread every minute they spend at the mic demonstrating *leadership*,
this new dread feeds on fish fingers and tortilla chips,
a magnum of Beaujolais ingested in the bath
while reading magazines about marathons,
you yearn after finish lines in foreign countries
bordering international cities made temporarily unreachable,
shelter in place is the same as age in place when you are this old,
pretend all can be made merry again, convince yourself,
sometimes some things take a little convincing
more than a normal number of naps,
extra snacks and a swarm of patience,
claw yourself out of this poorly caulked tub cleanly
and sleep uninterrupted for six to eight hours, maybe ten
if your bladder and the dogs co-operate,
there is nothing and no one standing in your way,
except capitalism and global pandemics,
a sinking feeling washes over you with every dark reminiscing,
your replay is all jammed up, old nights intentionally lit,
wandering through bars and backrooms, bumps and bathrooms,
sloppy drunk and ludicrous, much too loud music
thrumming away in your abdomen,
all that old passing out while life was passing by
keeps you awake at night anxious and wondering
did you miss all the good stuff while out searching for the good stuff
a thousand times found at the wrong party
where bloodhounds were set to a scent you never fully acquired a taste for,
everyone thought talking about art and literature was weird and boring,

because talking about art and literature was weird and boring for everyone
but you, all the while knowing nothing happens from the couch
and meeting no one online, you went out for ten,
maybe fifteen years, begrudgingly hoping
to find someone happy to stay home, pleased to rest alongside you,
watch a documentary, drink a hot toddy and sleep,
and now, sure, look! Holy thundering jesus,
tis magical stuff,
one can hardly believe the likes of it
as the whistle blew, while the clock ran down the road ahead of you,
yelling track, track! you burst free ahead, spit and blood and tears,
sheer unrelenting ragged determination
wanting something nice for yourself
you caught up to him or he to you,
who cares how we got here really,
two people fell into pace,
some modern-day miracle,
of timing and broken hearts,
you are some grateful to all the women
before you who did not make a lick of sense
you would have scorned all this as
old foolishness if it had been told to you,
you would have said tsk, tsk, that never happens in real life,
but it does and here goes as much as you can muster;
you decided to change and you changed,
so now be easy with yourself like a weary toddler
carried in from their car seat, be careful now,
be full of care.

EIGHTY YEARS OF AGE / EIGHTY-TWO FOR WOMEN

My father's first cousin died at fifty-three, his near
grown daughters I barely recognize as women.

Searching faces, scanning features,
seeking out smiles borrowed from their mothers,
gestures known are temporarily forgotten until
the lines along a jawbone fasten against the world,
fused solid, undeniable, earnest and angry.

This determination reminds me of myself,
an auntie or a cousin holding me up also as a child
to see if I was one of Nels' girls, look at dem
eyes, look, just the same weary watery blue,
the way she tilts her chin when she sulks,
same as her fadder luh, all the time tormented.

Likewise I put my finger on it, pin it down,
some familiar combination, realization firing, and these
girls/women/cousins are all at once kindred,
the little beauties and hardships we share amongst ourselves
like sour candies counted and shook out by a beloved bare palm
over the old shop counter, everything falls away
in the moments we are held fast again in grief,
we are one less than the day before.

This flood of everyone reluctantly bidding farewell
is a swamping, needlessly soaked in unfairness, satched,

there comes that homespun shudder, I touch my hand upon
the knot of temper knitting in my throat, knowing this weld
of rage and hurt is a binding beyond any surname
we parcel between generations.

I remember a dog. Angel.
Untrained and hyper, tethered to a spike in the ground,
watching children play, wanting to be free,
she chased us upon the family lands,
ignorant and half-foolish, wild with excitement,
her chain whipping behind her
down over the little grade I thought was
mountainous in my youth, how many times did I screech
afraid of the dog's bite having never been fully bitten
but well aware of fangs, fright collecting inside, a reservoir.

Dad says, never happened, he doesn't remember any
of this, he thinks the dog belonged to someone else's cousin.

Where did I get these heaving memories so thick and full-chested?

I remember the dog barking just beyond the grassy bank,
up on her hind legs watching me strike out, distracted and
worried something bad would happen for which I would be
blamed. But what did you do to make the dog bite you?

There was no concern back then for young dogs or girls
or even boys who drank more than men during times
when men weren't even meant to be drinking.

Canadian average life expectancy does not apply to my family tree.

When Dad calls me in the early morning
I start grieving at the sound of my own name.

Megan, it's Dad, your uncle, your cousin, a friend,
in the backyard, in the basement, over the side of the boat,
the doctor called us in the night and we drove fast over the
snowy roads, a parade of sorrow, saying goodbye in the dark.

Sometimes we didn't make it. Sometimes we were too late.

I learned to write letters at six to say *I miss you*
to my father's brother who at thirty-three had a brain
busy sprouting tumours. His son, our Rocky, went whitewater rafting.

A freak accident, the only person injured.
His mother kept his cat.

Not nearly long enough later she died of cancer months before retirement.
No one counts the funerals.

Our island is caught in perpetual mourning of collectively felt premature death.

I would rather we'd our people back than this wealth of resilience.

Or what time remained of our childhoods
had we not been steady marching out the graveyard road
wishing farewell to pieces of ourselves going forever
underground in glossy boxes lined in blue and pink.

I don't see god inside this poem or any poem.

I don't see god inside any words laid down on paper.

Perhaps that makes me no poet but a fisherman's daughter still.

HOUSEPLANTS AND HOUSE CATS

Clip a piece
of yourself off
like a houseplant
the cat gnawed on all winter.

You, too, can be reborn in water.

A glass on the windowsill can do a lot of growing.

It's like this,
a few short days ago,
this new plant was nothing,
worse, a worn half-eaten wreck
gnawed to bring bile up on the carpet,
but you never mind what was before now
the past is teaching you adaptation,

all things long suffering from envy
and greedy esteem
can be revived.

Fresh air, sunshine, concern.

Turn yourself skyward,
the act of arching up alone
demonstrates commitment to change.

You knows now yourself how
a fine day on clothes feels like balm
upon a sore face pockmarked from interference.

Stop picking at yourself like that, you'll scar!

Take every inch of the good you got left
trim your stalks back to what is decent,
the whole parts, the before-you-got-cut-up-
and-tattered parts,
sever them parts and be fresh,
hole up from sick-feeling felines
hoping to ease their own sour insides by
tearing some off you, sure girl, listen here,
kittens don't know any better than that,
kindles are born destructive,
how long have you been sitting
there
with that cat on your lap
afraid to move.

Stand up for yourself.

Slip yourself clear of cat traps
rooms full of brown tips,
dry rot holding
perishing colours.

Fill every room, all available space will bloom
new greens, if you keep at it — hang in there,

this is long-game stuff now,
preening and plucking free the wilting bits,
pinching deadheads between your nails,
turning toward sunbeams for balance,
pressing fingers into the topsoil,
your cousin hates the word *moist*,
and so you said it gratuitously when she annoyed you,
this is in the new plant too, this and all the plants
that died during that time, words
can't even keep a plant alive,
your old condemnation changes,

there will be flowers.

USE IT OR LOSE IT

Our father seeds evidence
of his labour about my meagre inheritance
showcasing his intent to manage
this birthright house
indefinitely.

He will place an outport
in any field bearing his surname,
two tow sleighs sitting idle by,
the shiny plastic red gleaming backside
up and abandoned against the grown
green and grassy yard, forcing all
to mow around his claim.

Bait-boxes gate the store entrance,
a weather-worn rope handle hauling it closed
feels only the moment of release when giving way,
its threaded spine tugged-clear upon after decades
of yanking.

A lot is said in a breath of not speaking.

Opportunities to improve this bristly closure
presented themselves
year after year
until it ceased being a later decision
put off for another time or forgetfulness,

instead becoming
identity-hardened against the wind and debt,
having no latch, it fused with self and salvation,
everyone bellowing into the brush and bog
we don't want for better 'round here
we make do with what is handy
and mind our own business
which is no business of yours at all
you who we determine arbitrarily not of us.

Yet a few outliers, yourself included, are left
insisting we're all the same crowd sure
off the same boat landed on the same shore
my great-great-great English grandmother
is a Scotswoman in disguise same
as yours and his too, the works of us,
one side hiding Duncans,
another hiding Browns,
truth be told
(when someone is brave enough to tell it)
there was only one name written in each ledger
and from there on joined forever with the other only
names, not many, just enough to claw out a living
with whom we found already on their original path northward,
the emotional work of pulling us back together
is a burden best borne in short spurts to prevent exhaustion,
when aunties on all sides draw imaginary lines
of kinship with talk of
you knows now what they're like
and what we're like

as if there is innate difference
when rightly we're one collection of unwanted
generations tied together upon a rock cliff
sured up, desperate wedlock sought to multiply
a steady supply of womenfolk for the marriage bed
men for the boat and wood cut
and what lies between us
are the lies we tell ourselves about
this cove and that cove being formed
from some other when our shared relations
knit us into close quarters, no one is talking about
incest here, so you never mind the word you fear,
it is trenched in the graveyard two hundred years
apart atop French guardians, furriers and foes,
likely over the rightfully buried,
grave markers having been
robbed and then forgot,
who is to say where anyone is laid out for rest
no one knows their own mind anymore but you.

Hand-washing supper dishes in Palmolive
soap so plentiful and vibrant,
high suds slurping against
the grey sink lip, the smell of them
a clean remembrance,
the scent of your childhood
from the angle where Nanny stood in her pinny,
looking beyond the kitchen taps you
take your turn staring upon the ground where
once you flopped and held your water.

Beyond glass and
over a little rib of mire
tilts a rusted hot water boiler
supposed to serve some re-purpose,
listing heavy upon a lobster shoot
full-up of wet-rot from wintering outside,
bowing in on itself, garbage
for the regional collector who is rarely called
on for stuff around the door,
no one can tell anyone
what they can or cannot do on their own land
which is owned by the queen's imperial fantasies,
daydreams and lusted-after realities, her
common wealth never having been shared commonly or at all.

Allies coast to coast ignore
who got the goods, made off with the loot,
while grieving ongoing displacement,
a collection of hungry sharks is called a frenzy
and we feast on whoever's in reach
rather than gnaw the rolling heads of grander houses
than our own, nothing is more baffling
than poor girls of all colours
weeping over royal weddings, gasping
in admiration at the decadent footwear their
breaking backs bear
as the wildly well-heeled continue climbing
staircases to elevations beyond all measurable accounting
what is left after extraction is hate-filled feuding
declarations of what is and isn't ours.

Battles declared with a wheelbarrow,
old nets, industry gear of all invention
can be seen from every vantage
grasping at specks of what is left of us
we are still fishing here, the ensemble barks,
we are still working people homesteaded to this place,
the chorus cries mix with curses and calls for violence,
how we've come to this is so intangible,
undefinable, a shameful estimation
we were told to estimate as shameful.
Knowing what waste-landing will come
in the stead of visible usage,
our small residencies spread themselves upon the ground
leaving desperate allowance of belonging,
the coastline worn through with our despair,
tuckamore now torn by the bike tread
proclaiming movement between settlements
every edge lined with wood, tight and tidy
piled, each woodsman weary of the northwest
side of the house what for the cold-water waste.

Just over yonder a camper saved
for sometime-use over to Labrador
sinks into the groundwater,
everything is starting to falter
and give way under the pressure
of our weighted existence, the front end of her
seeping into the weary, satched-in runoff.

Your cousin's young man's
ambitions remain a ditch dug

where he wished to build a home
though no foundation ever lay upon the gap,
just a hole filling in again,
all there is of it now is hogweed and hemlock,
little purple flowers never named though beloved
enough we once plucked multitudes
from the swampy earth
as gifts for our moms and grandmothers,
a display of girlhood, womanliness taking back
drudged out parcels of cove handed over
from one man to another until no brothers
were born, or stayed, to receive them
as is the case with us.

IN CASE OF EMERGENCY

There's a decaying empire on our doorstep
purchased from repo during the last capital failure.

This was the nineties, a time before my urban time.

Townies tell stories of shuttered storefronts along the barren downtown
as our cod moratorium rolled up on the fashion district
no one hauled on occasion-rubbers to run down
into the beach beef bucket in hand
for this puny offering reeking of
baymen and desperation and tags.

Got to get me stamps b'y.

I have just the one memory of us here, lost in a maze of one-ways,
my father swearing and sweating once found accidentally off the parkway.

I dare say they'll steal the hubcaps clean off the car.

Unease undoes our fathers and we are quiet daughters in the wake of fury.

The bones in my toes are crooked, see.

I had been wearing my aunt's hand-me-down broomball shoes,
using her hand-me-down stick, thacking along,
the orange rubber pinching me
as I raced 'round the rink already full feet ahead of her.

Nan says, my look've the size of her!
I am the tallest girl child, tallest grandchild, then,
she there worried all the right sizes would be too dear for me.

Our small-boned matriarch plotted ways to contain my big bones.

A cousin wraps her delicate hand around my wrist to prove me huge.
Look, she says, her thin thumb and forefinger hardly overlap.

Years later I will use pictures, past and present, to gauge myself.

Regardless, I ask for larger shoes because I want to be fast,
strong, unstoppable, I want to score, I want my father cheering from the stands.

I am instructed to make them last another year.

Or not play.

And so we learn to move through pain.

You cannot manage money you don't have.

Not playing, being no option ever entertained, this fish swam to the sides of her
tank, grew against the glass, wiggling past the pressing threat of implosion, there
was pushback, to this day, ossein turns in on itself.

The podiatrist said bones need space to grow straight.

FRESH NEOLIBERALS

Declaring capitalism
suddenly works
because it suddenly works
for you
is a sellout move selling out quick
for the first cash in hand on offer,
saying nothing at the mic leaves
everything left unsaid,
you're all talk
and no substance sure.
When we found out the fix was in
you were For. Your. Self.
For getting yours
forgetting
every other former you
still living in the yesterday
you left behind in the dirt
kicked clear your boot bottom,
look of the shine on you now,
gleaming,
against the snotty nose you once
rubbed raw with a shirt sleeve
pulled off the bedroom floor,
no bother even smelling it,
knowing well enough it's not been washed,
mom said, *what doesn't go in the laundry basket*
stays dirty

and by god, by-gone you
never listened to anything mom said
what did she know anyway, she was
just your mother,
can't take her with you, best leave her behind
with all the other relations denied your kinship.
Don't talk to anyone from home anymore
pronounced with too much pride and nare
trace of h'an h'accent
soon as you got a spot of polish
on your shoes,
you pay a man to buff that binding
now except to occasionally
play pretend-poor when it suits you,
a scatter time you mentions
an affiliation to this place you never
visit and regularly swear off as backward,
full of idiots, inbreds and rednecks you don't like
who don't like you much either.
Jealous! Jealous! you bawl, They're all jealous of me!
cause you some great big deal on the mainland,
#nobigdeal but really really in actual fact
you thinks yourself huge, everyone can tell
by how you speaks to them
or don't
as the case may be, see,
tis not about your bank account
so much as about the company
you keeps with bankers,
people don't much mind if you lives below

the Bay Street sign which got fuck all to do with
the sour taste upon their tongues smerting
from your revulsion for how you got made,
the stench of humiliation and aspiration mixes
to reek from out your pores like a slow rot
near on boiling, if I can smell you coming,
then everyone can smell you coming
which is mighty off-putting for the off-spring
your fast crawl toward the social up-fall
sets an example for
everyone and all of us still on our knees,
begging for some salvageable share
to improve this standard of living
and no, I never said you alone
was responsible for solidarity
but hear me now,
the blame I am laying at your feet
is yours,
you earned it each time you turned the
conversation toward congenial
when a point was in the making
without your assistance or help at all,
we never expected you to stand up to the man,
what with your well-aligned genitalia, wait,
I mean, agenda,
but by the thundering jesus,
do not be interrupting disrupters
whose disruption reared and raised you,
never mind stepping atop sore shoulders
with your pissy privilege cleats on

you long ago rose from the carnage
screaming *Don't look back!*
Never look back!
Run!
as if old labour might catch
this tiger by the tail and pin you in place
stuck forever sitting at the lowly island table
nibbling the less than lunch afforded you by birth
you cannot abscond this rank cafeteria
with chipped trays and food frays
for fancy party clothes in penthouses
with chandeliers gilded in gold
and remain seated at the same table
you cannot shit on your cake
and gorge on it too.

BREATHLESSNESS

Those who've never held their breath claim
health is all about breathing air deep into the body,
not semi-regular facials or store-bought berries filling the fridge,
not wood-burning fireplaces blazing, cords cut and delivered a panful
to a time by some aged bayman found on Kijiji, bit of cash,
Christmas presents for the grandkids he buys himself now the wife passed,
side hustles under the table and untaxed, hidden from the same greedy fuckers
who sign grand holiday bonuses for their friends before attending parties
in special-built, designer dream homes, awards galore,
and where did all the money go, brass placards on the doorstep proclaiming:
it is here, see, look, look up, turn your face toward that vaulted ceiling and admire
the overhead space in their great rooms, the chandelier declares itself,
one of many, skimmed off the charity top all in the name of humanity,
memorials and saviour trips travelled by the politically hopeful,
legacy spawn and whatever homegrown celebrity can be found
to endorse them, it's a good gig if you say nothing of consequence
and smile a lot, joke or sing a tune, free champagne eases self-disgust
sliding down the gullet as the PR machine runs fast ahead of any possible
epiphanies; marketing teams create new groundbreaking, trailblazing, pivoting
prizes for the papers to talk about, give 'em something to push around,
the 24 cycle spins, headshots, memoirs, ghostwriters never named,
likely females with little choice and no childcare, while barely a whiff is written
about stealing from the sick, the poor, the elderly, hustlers and villains
cannot be put off the smoked salmon flown in from Alaska,
fundraisers secretly raising funds straight from the public purse
for elections scarcely called before the vote is in and everyone is aghast
with the stupidity of our southern neighbours when all around them

tiny trumps play their stacked kitties like they came by these cards
dealt on merit rather than receiving gifts from their fathers who
stood witness at the judge's wedding, and tell me again now
how the laws are made to benefit our equal wellness, mention
another time how breathing into my diaphragm will correct the
hateful disparity between my shallow gasp, the lungs of our people and
those reared high to squeeze us 'round the middle till we surrender or choke.

TWENTY-THREE-DOLLAR MIMOSAS

I will stop talking about inequality at brunch
when brunch stops being so fucking unequal

In Vancouver, power shaves gold flakes onto the
cream puffs while people overdose in the streets

A millennial was murdered downtown and
a local celeb tweeted to save one dog in Toronto

The *Globe and Mail* wants a fluff piece so I talk
endlessly about inner-city youth and racial slurs

I cannot even claim *I'm poisoned* in outrage anymore
as local politicians sanction sacrificing the water table

The fossil-fuel horse you're riding will soon buck you
clear to the ground to be needlessly trampled

I don't even want to forget the cost of living while the
cost of living kills everyone found unable to afford it

I see you deciding every day to do nothing at all
good with your access and I reject this shit strategy.

A PIANO IN THE SUNROOM

All I wanted as a girl was a piano
and a house big enough to home it,
dogs asleep on the rugged floor.
For me, reading music was a new idea
in my place where reading words had
just caught on. I know how it hurts
to watch others from elsewhere
enjoy your home better than yourself,
the pains of rage welling inside, flush,
we barely had trains to take before they
hauled up the tracks, we grabbed our
last coppers as keepsakes, tried to claw
back pieces of ourselves that still felt like
ourselves, before we were renamed:
province. Remember, root cellars
were our playrooms, the dank smell
inside the hovelled-out door, familiar.
Your old uncle warning of insecurity,
claiming it will all have to be torn down,
recall the teepees of cut wood drying
ring-round the cove, an accordion lodged
near the knitting basket on the floor, or
Nanny's needles struck straight through
the join where the clasp gave way for wear,
these socks darned to death by your grandmother
were crafted special to match your winter coat

perfectly, convinced everything is worth saving,
anything that was beautiful once
can be made pretty again.

GROWN-UP BOY COUSINS

You heart Oil & Gas.
But Oil & Gas does not heart you back.
I'm not trying to be mean. Or nothing. Start
some new feud or carry-on. What I mean to say is, it can't.

A commercial sector does not feel human because a commercial
sector is not human. It's commercial. Exploiting and distracting you
from being yourself, the you that is experience, memory, expectation,
vulnerable under those company coveralls, the living spit and piss, fragile you.

No industry will grieve your broken body, toll the bells on your expiration day.
Your decline is for concealing, dinged-up machinery you are. Replaceable. A tool
for easy use. If Oil & Gas could pay you nothin, they would pay you nothin.
If it could work you harder, longer, still, it would do that, too.

Destructive industry cannot feel you, do you feel me?

It will be my tears and the tears of our people, old and aging,
winded and windowless, coned in pollution, lesions all along our insides.
It will be us, scraped together. It will be everyone, left to suffer.
It will be your own kin and comrades that will once again salt the ground
through to brined when the company breaks your bones or your spirit.

Whatever comes first comes first. They don't give a shit for you.

This is war stuff you're after getting into for dollar-dollar bills, big trucks and
lip-service from men you barely know, trauma bonding you to a steel platform

or tailing pond crusted over in dead birds, some shocking morbid
sight that is. Look what you're after doing, look at it.
If you are not scared by the fires daily burning
you are not feeling all your feelings,
turn yourself back on me b'y, feel the fleshy bits that make you
man, do not worry over what comes, if awareness brings a flooding,
know I will wipe your snotty nose with my sleeve like when we were children.

Men should cry. Some things are worth crying over.
Weep for your youngsters, your mother, your pop and your wife.
Ache for who you wanted to be when you grew up. Mourn that guy.

Or change for him.

Sure, the rigging 'round the drill shaft never even asked your
last or real name, no one wants to know victim details.

You don't need to be a kid to be kidnapped.

Speak up in a new voice, yell your own name again, start feeling
yourself, you are no cookie, toolpush, worm or finger, you are more,
you are a lot, these hitches collecting you like roughnecks void of ambition
boil you down to what you can buy instead of who you are or should be.

Hear me out: you owes them nothing. You can leave. You can be different.

But if you don't, or won't, or can't, hear this too: hating your industry
does not mean I love you any less. Just that I hate them more
for limiting how you value yourself because you
are so valued by me. Remember:

your body was forged along the watershed
where we watched weasels weave the wharf boulder-side,
we slashed sharp rocks against dock rocks to mine their
spoils believed to hold crystals, treasures, convinced
there had to be something more than nothing,
we did that, our spry imaginations yet unspoilt by the limiting
notions of profit, we explored ideas, options of becoming,
wanting to be someone else before being told we could be ourselves.

Because who we are is good enough. No proof of purchase necessary.

You are good enough as you are. Were always good enough for us.

FLORIDA

The man who will be your father-in-law
does not know he is the man
who will be your father-in-law, yet,
you are still New Girlfriend, not to be mistaken for
Old Girlfriend or Ex Girlfriend or even
Favourite Girlfriend,
there was that other one,
remember her, what was her name,
Rebecca or Tiffany, Jennifer, Amanda was it,
studied education, went to nursing school, became
a doctor or a dentist, something equally respectable,
you though, you've opinions galore on topics
wide-ranging: single-use plastics, world politics,
refined sugar and housing,
anything briefly mentioned on BBC, honestly,
if you bit your tongue
every time it needed biting,
you'd've bitten it clean off by now,
then you'd have no tongue to speak with so
not starting stuff is a non-starter,
you tried censorship once before to serve a man
you liked less and then — not much at all,
running out in anger, embarrassment and financial ruin,
as such you've wholly abandoned the muzzle for the mic.

Sarasota, Tampa Bay, where are them Siesta Keys at?

Just beyond this sea of cars and trucks, jeeps and SUVs,
a single-file flood of impatience is pooling.

Put everything back the way you found it does not apply to everything.

Cherokee Park, South Poinsettia, Indian Beach, Sapphire Shores —

and everyone dreams of manatees

while trapped in endless sprawl,
pawn-shop signs red line the lengthy
four-lane where mobile homes
sun their backsides.

Every passing vehicle close-on
smacks a trailer on the ass for being a trailer
unable to afford a fence, gates, trees,
the thin windows shake, a quiver
you well remember, the wind against the glass,
the draft held between the panes, suddenly dampered,
your aunt sneaking smokes out the crack,
this was back when cool aunts still snuck smokes,
your nan fast asleep in the rocking chair
pretended to be fast asleep in the rocking chair,
Dad another time with a dart between his lips,
the metal clasp against the frame unclipped to smoke
and knit headings in the kitchen, his chair leaning
back on the mustard coloured fridge to just see
the CBC evening news on the living room TV.

You try to write a poem about your father before
realizing all these poems are about your father.

All sound and sense in your mobile home
was drowned out by the northeaster
rattling them shit windows in their casings
and your parents rowing over the chequebook.

Down south they shudder the same sad shudder,
the curtains sway inside with the motor vehicle tide
even though every window is fastened in place,
not going anywhere, you lot aren't,
held tight against all this freedom, you wonder
if they sleep in the front where the hitch pitches from
the underbelly ever-ready for a pluck that never comes,
claiming we could flee is a facade,
these are not vacation homes, this everyday
driveway splits from the strip by that mangy slick
of tanning grass no sprinkler can green against the
exhaust fumes pluming every pathway toward the sand.

Guns! Guns! Guns! for sale everywhere in all directions,
as if you might forget for a second to arm yourself,
the largest star-spangled flag flies over an Italian luxury
car dealership because this is AMERICA motherfucker
get ready for the class race / fast pace / gender war
everyone is so nearly lit, even the commercials are
smouldering, the AC pumps cool air in and you fear
all humans other side the glass divided by design,
we all wait for the lights to turn, the cars

idling near us may well be full of hitmen, maybe you're
just a scaredy-cat, forever pemishing, lick your paws and soothe
yourself as birds are flipped all ways from Fridays by angry humans
flying nowhere, always drive with both hands on the wheel, there
is a gas station here and here and here and here,
you do not want to break down on this highway.

A blue-and-yellow playpen sits outside a screen door,
it thankfully does not contain a baby,
you are so relieved no Black or Brown child
is peering at you from inside its toxic container,
there are poor white people here, too,
the not-poor-white-people-here say,
you could reply, I know,
I was one of those where we come from,
but that's a lot and you're a lot already.

This is your first American beach, you don't count Hawaii,
Florida is your first true capital C Capitalism beach,
it is nothing like European and Asian waterfronts,
seagulls plunge-dive into laps stealing french fries,
women in visors and sunscreen squeal over the theft,
no one bothers the bag of fruit between your lounge chairs,
nothing you eat is like a hot dog or hamburger, your food is unrecognizable
to these feathered foragers, every little party has one beach blanket
and three DJs, they loudly FaceTime family in New Jersey,
Look! Look where we are! We're at the beach!
The phone scans the vista of thousands of people
standing in water to their shins, not swimming.
Your man is reading the sports section of a local paper and

a book about talking to strangers you will never talk to,
half-heartedly eating fistfuls of dried figs and catnapping.
You hate this fucking beach but you have never been happier.

OVER AND OVER AND OVER AGAIN, WE LET IT ALL GO

Repetitive actions in animals indicate boredom
or brain damage. The security man at Costco draws a slash
through our receipt seconds after scanning the cart
for pretense. Risk assessments by the PUB all pass
inspection without a hitch and every small-town doctor
at the clinic is told that the old couple eats good as good goes
undefined. Also told: no one is poor or stressed and the cod is coming
back. Now more than ever! You watch and witness self-deceit.
It's the scientists who're lying. They lied in the past,
what makes you think they are truth-tellers now?
The Oil & Gas companies are looking out for your nan's best interest,
for sure, for sure, corporations are people and the 1% are the smartest,
most generous humans, angels really, definitely heroes amongst us.
It's buddy on income support with no education and neither
skill but for his ability to shake a bit of gear to he's friends,
he's the real enemy of the people, lock him up,
throw his youngsters in foster care. The slumlord millionaire
who patches rot holes with lumberyard scraps drives a Mercedes
through his own neighbourhood and a rusted-out pickup
through yours, even got a poverty disguise, denim on denim
over an old white Molson T-shirt free from the beer box.
What? No, you're right, these are not perfect
thoughts because I am not a perfect person.
Would you prefer something polished? So would I
but what I got was what I got and what you get of me is this:
a beautiful young lawyer once told me to leave politics
to the politicians who pay her, our friends sexually assault us

105

in our apartments and then ask for a ride home, walking in the snowy street
is found too dangerous for grown men but safe enough for children,
preventable damage is preventable only if it is labelled damage,
call your ex what he really was and he will stop stalking you, maybe even
cease grooming young women and emailing them his non-apologies, moral weaklings
do not deserve forgiveness or acceptance or time, if a question is being avoided,
keep asking that question, the person talking down to you is scared you
will speak up, lift your eyes, make sustained contact.
Hold them there, in your view, to account.

OUR FATHER IS SICK

We know it is serious because he quit smoking.

The doctor in our northern region thinks it is
thyroid related
prescribes a minuscule increase in meds.

This does nothing
to improve his worsening situation.

It worsens.

Could be heart disease.
Could also be cancer.
Could be a great number of things
they have not screened for because they lack the capacity to screen
for a great number of things at this, or any time
in the place where we were made.

Our father is sixty-four and believes he must live with this or die.

Only his daughters ask why he has it,
how he got it, what triggered this recent bout of illness.
Though no one bothers answering his daughters
we need not or cannot be answered.

We are an unanswerable quartet of female detectives,
like toddlers having newly acquired language,

we voice our whys in rapid and overlapping succession
such as to exhaust all "adults" in the room
who have long since stopped
demanding explanations.

Many of them without agency to request clarification
for fear speaking up might reveal some
innate inferiority
as if all should be expected to
know everything about everything.

Knowledge less than absolute knowledge
is deemed to be evidence of hereditary ignorance
which leads them down the garden path toward further
humiliation and dependency.

Besides, innocent
whys vocalized in youth
were often met with
because I said so.

Accepted as the word of god
or otherwise tanned out of them by some
man's leather, a father's belt or teacher's strap.

Authority has no use of our collective desire for meaning-making.

It impedes *progress of industry* and so many vulnerable people,
like my father's vulnerable people, were silenced.
They swallowed down a lifetime of whys and worries

internalizing every suspicion that they were not being treated right
without the words to articulate their feelings and concerns.
They turned it inward.

Internalization requires a lot of space in the body.
It overtakes you. The body is overtaken.

I left home to study intergenerational trauma,
ecological grief and exploitation.

Irony here would be funny
if our relative living condition
wasn't nightmarishly common.

It is hard to track and yet nothing at all.
No one counts funerals around here.

Yes, I said it again so you would hear it twice.

Hardly the tip of the iceberg our alleyway is infamous for.
Barely a breath of tragedy. A puff of it as we hold air
in, every exhale feels like possibly losing another parent or sibling.

I have been told that we do not breathe deeply enough.
Our bodies are starved for oxygen,
we hold old fumes in the lungs.
What is needed to refresh does not reach our cells.
We are forever quietly hyperventilating through our short lives,
fully reactive and ready to detonate.
Nan turned eighty-one April Fool's Day to her own great surprise.

She does not know what to eat anymore. Nothing agrees with her.
Says nothing sits right in her belly but unfairness of which she is full-up, thanks.

Nan believes the government will come right through her house if ever they
wants to, that they will split her home down the middle if there was something
of value found beneath it.

She uses violent language like *Tear her wide open* and *asunder*.
Nan only knows what the TV tells her of rape culture
but her vocabulary is steeped in it like a tea bag she continuously returns to
regardless of fading flowerless flavour.

I once witnessed a bureaucrat at crown lands counsel an elderly couple
against deeding their homestead, claiming it's just a piece of paper,
doesn't mean anything around the bay.

I watched them worry aloud about their children's inheritance as
this middle-aged, middle-class-educated, urban man claimed
they've no such rights to title.
And then I watched him lean hard on how costly and complicated
the process will be, application fees, surveys, declaring it a waste of time and money.

Industry will come for everything it wants with its jaws open.

This man is the agent of industry.
It is called crown lands for a reason.

The Oil & Gas bailout PR is full-on propaganda.
The new first-ever female university president of mixed heritage
is on the line claiming we're *intrinsically linked* to the energy sector.

All of this is lies but so few people are well enough to recognize any harm in the deceit.
The fix was always in.

We can all be deemed pollutable.
Anywhere decided a wasteland.
It is but a conference call away.

When I was little,
they burned the garbage
across from the health clinic
where my young mother worked.

We drove through the incinerator plume
on our way home from hockey, everyone pinching
their noses to prevent the stink. The new school and elder-care facility
now lies on the site. They added the new health clinic to the lot.
A grey box turned from all views of the ocean which we are meant to forget.
Our ill, nearly everyone now, regardless of age or income,
go there to sit in a stuffy room awaiting new prescriptions.
The doctors tell them to keep doing what they are doing. Or don't.

Our father continues to eat a bowl of Cinnamon Toast Crunch every day for breakfast.

My anguish grows.

The hurt I got inside my body gives me goosebumps on my legs.

SILLY BITCHES, TRUCKS ARE FOR BIG BOYS

Still now, I dream of murderers
found standing in the hallway after
having, in my temporary relief,
forgotten to lock every latch.
Like a lazy barn cat sunning
in a sunspot, I lost track
of my foes. Assuming far-
flung movement or immobility
would overtake vigilance,
I ignored time and place
passing between us, so pleased
was I, with the happy moments
collecting on the fridge door
like cooling custards on the counter,
until the triggers flash to find one,
or all, reappearing in my mind's
eye disturbed by dislocation,
realizing much much later, I had
caught glimpses of cars from the
corner visor slow-coasting by
as I whitewashed the front
steps on a summer Saturday morning
clocking no conclusions until these
idle machines are spotted again
housing human-looking ghosts.
I dream intruders stand alongside

our bed inspecting, for morbid
delight and judgment, our framed
photos, nighttime reading, discarded
clothing upon the floor, a peach
slipper visible beneath the black dog's
chin who sleeps near enough
to sense us breathing through
the night. I imagine these wrong
men live inside me, and every
wounded female body full-up
of their rage, having gathered confidence
from one another, the government,
economics and random trucks upon
the highway, their message blaring
with each close call, we are less
than human, what of our justified fears,
we know to shake the knob to ensure
it has a hold of itself, where even a tinted
rear window decal calls women silly bitches
for nothing and no good reason like
it is funny, a great good joke to tell. Haha
escapes me when the air is constantly
kicked out 'cause I worry worry worry
myself over delusions of all the desperate
men who hurt us, now fired from their jobs,
relearning the language of destruction
having nothing new to do with their extra
time after losing all and easy access
to a host of prey-things, play-things,

spit and loathing seeping from
their grey and wilting bodies,
the answer, though, is no,
you do not get to come back.

DON'T EAT THE CHIPS

I used to date drinkers and loners,
sea-salt-and-vinegar types,
burn the mouth right off ya,
keep you coming back for more, yelling,
Get the chip bowl clear of me for fuck sake,
'fore I makes myself sick again!
Couldn't help it, was reared on
harsh words, sparse rewards and junk.
Dad threatening to give me a thump
upside the head half the time for existing
the way I was made. He couldn't help it neither,
he was taught women were seen and not heard
and there I stood forever talking, words escaping, even now,
steady as freshwater runoff after the spring thaw, rippling forth relentless,
demanding attention with my presence in this or that room,
sure, flicking my hair around and narrowing my eyes
over questionable comments at the dinner table.
I don't know my place because no place was made for me,
the one speaking role for a woman was filled by daughters
of better breeding, slight accents and perfect teeth.
So I spent time with men who spoke sullenly of themselves
like they were children still, men who felt already faded,
washed-out ghosts, limp and wounded by the culture shift, depleted
and without hope, they saw nothing between the cradle and the grave,
no easy glory presented itself like endless plates of cookies in the rec room,
didn't even learn to look up from the game to say *Gee thanks Mom.*

Ask for a drink though, and then another, some thirsty b'y, parched.
The prematurely withered bathed in the potential of young women,
diligent and promising, sincere, sweet-smelling, satched.
They whispered weasel words into ears, leaning in the
corners of dark bars, across a pool table or
even a desk, there is nowhere safe
to be clever and appealing.
Young Burt Reynolds meets the Night Stalker
and we're all gorging ourselves on fifty shades of
serial killer, eyes full of malicious intent or wet blinkers
brimming with self-pity. No one could tell me just
as no one can tell any lonesome woman,
trust amongst girls is rough-cut and unsupported,
learned suspicion and crafted competition,
I could not be warned off,
having learned my caretaker role early on,
surviving on the sting of neglect,
familiar as an old photograph or my mother's
inability to remember me as a child, maybe that was you
or maybe it was your sister, whole childhoods lost
and forgotten, my rose-coloured glasses were crushed
underfoot in the first fast move. No one bought me a new pair,
there wasn't extra at the time which is well and good enough,
there is no luxury in misremembering yourself,
just mindless echoes, myths of self-destruction and regret.
Baby relations, please: do not replicate our misdeeds,
do not date men like we dated because we dated them, bad boys
are just bad, breakups are not endorsements or female failures but opportunities
to shift, transformation is a series of small corrections, surely I have made many,

will likely make more still, and though you cannot hear my words, I beseech you
nonetheless, know: it is not for you to fix some other damaged human,
the only happiness you are responsible for is your own.

SALT-STAINED THROUGH

Here is a part of the story you don't know.
I did not inherit my grandmother's house from my grandmother.
It was left to the estate. My father and his siblings,
spread across Newfoundland and the country we call Canada,
were willed the worth of it. Though they hadn't privilege enough
to care for the beloved shell of our bygone livelihoods,
as they were far too furious with the busy work of living.
Revolving economic disasters steady occupied
the passing of their growing adult days.
They kept the lights on, they kept the truck going.
We were reared up smart and sturdy, Coles,
as the gale force wind and freezing rain went on lashing Nanny's house.
We lost track of each other in the time shift,
moved further afield by out-migration, education, desperation,
even death. And as we ebbed and flowed from the cove,
the tides turned over. Our family home fell into disrepair.
We watched it falling. Took pictures of the fallen bits upon the firm and frozen ground.
Documenting pieces of ourselves like paint chips peeling from the clapboard.
The porch, having blown open one winter, smelled of wet rot.
Our school photos still hung in frames on the warped-papered walls.
What a sin, we said, what a sin for us.
Cousins whispered about the state of it
while drinking beers under blankets on the couch.
There were murmurs amongst the older lot. The house, they said,
would have to be torn down. So I asked for it.
From Montreal, I wrote a letter.
Begged my elders for the little biscuit box out on the point.

I was twenty-five and penniless. One day I would be neither, I promised them,
and we would all wish after Nanny's sitting room then.
What do you want that for, Meggie, they wondered aloud,
worried that I was wading in over my boots.
Me: their well-known and much-loved boot-soaker.
But they gave me my way. And Dad allowed me to foremen us into my thirties,
tearing the tiny house back to her studs. Frantically gathering up small pockets of funds,
progress always held up by my bank account. This year, the doors and windows.
Next year, the siding. Electrical upgrades are some dear.
In and out of the poor house strutted my stubborn nature.
And there were times when I thought, what have you done?
When I thought, you are held here now.
When I thought, this is much too much rowing with your father.
But I did what I did because I knew then as I do now
that I have always been held to this present rowing over the past
to make up the future with my father. That we are bound to the cove and to each other
and to the whole of our fierce family like carbon fast-fixed in the rough rock we
survive upon.
And I am so proud of these people who somehow made themselves up on this point
nine miles from the mainland, facing North America, yet a world away.
So it is that when I am heart-hurt, wounded or weary,
when I forget myself and feel afraid,
I drive an entire day's length to Savage Cove.
The place where I made myself up, too.
And I sleep in my little blue bedroom, in my little green house,
so I can wake to the same crisp morning light that woke my grandmother.
I do this to remember her, myself, who we are and who we can be
on our Great Northern Peninsula.

NANNY'S HOUSE

I do not write in public because I cannot write in public.
That is the truth of it. I do not have the capacity to avert stimuli.
I am programmed open-tuned.
Constantly seeking and searching out frequencies in any shared space.
All detectable stations layer outlandishly over the words in my mind.
It gets loud. Textured.
A late-night radio antenna grabbing signals from neighbouring towns,
I pick up story-waves ceaselessly.
Everything is important and impossible to filter.
When without choice, I find myself plucking at lonely syllables
in cafés and airports wondering after what is mine.
I want not to mistake what is someone else's for my own.
I purposefully try to hold distance between myself and others
to prevent this unintended bleed.
Because I absorb conflict.
This happens most when I am forced to write near other humans.
I take them in. I take them on. Some writers find this helpful.
They enjoy additional. I do not. I am too porous for extra.
My head is ready-made noisy. I need quiet and routine.
Two sleeping dogs in an empty room, at least,
in an empty house around the bay,
better yet. Family and friends near but
separate from me while I lose myself in crafting sentences.
One after the other after the other.
I am not present during these working hours. I am elsewhere.
Sometimes I look up to discover myself still in my bathrobe,
the late afternoon light picking apples across the tablecloth.

But there are new pages. Often many.
This privacy is a lot to ask of everyone, I know,
but it is usually a lot I am asking of myself.
And I read my work aloud. No one needs or wants to witness that.
My frustrated rage and bluster-weeping would put anyone off their sandwich.
The salty cursing would cause many a grandfather to coughing-spit their tea.
It is a courtesy that I write in seclusion.
I'm doing Newfoundland a favour
composing the hardest bits of everything in my little house
in our little cove on the northernmost part of the island where every room
feels like having one's back to the wall looking out upon the page.
This place inherited from my kin, surrounded by all my relations, is my safe space.
We made it altogether in sturdy offering.
It was and remains a steady collective contribution
as we remember time spent in childhood.
Named for Nanny brim full to bursting with memories.
My father in his gear shed talking to whichever uncle has swung by, their truck
in full view from the kitchen window where I collect another cup of coffee,
woodsmoke rising from the stove.
My mother on her lunch break standing against the door jamb
in her work clothes asking after my word count.
A cousin on the phone. She has made a pot of soup.
Drop over sure for a bowl if you gets hungry.
Your Aunt Millie will bring one over to ya if you're too busy. Just text.
Everyone letting me alone while constantly checking in.
They know I am in there writing. They don't need to see it to believe it.
This makes me feel trusted and beloved. Later,
I will walk the dogs out the graveyard road headlong into the easterly blast
to set them free bouncing upon the bog spongy underfoot.
This is where I first learned to think up stories in the blowing silence.

It is where I do my best work.

Raincoat. Rubber boots. Gloved hands in May.

Without witness, void of display, out of earshot.

This is what I mean when I say solitude.

I have always been wary of open offices dismissing vulnerability.

As a child, I did not like it when the teacher stood behind my chair full of expectation.

I do not like being hovered over still. I resent unnecessary supervision.

I lean toward resistance.

Resist these phantom feelings evoking every boss you ever had

gritting their teeth while breathing down your neck in tandem for effect.

Willing you to think faster, write better, sit straighter in your chair,

make them rich and popular, all before five o'clock.

Ignoring your discomfort. The nerves in your belly.

Counting how many times you pee.

Pretending this new way of working works for everyone

when it clearly does not work for you.

They've proven that now, too.

This thing the body always knew.

Some of us need a door to think behind.

And the option to open and close it.

VAGUELY ASHBERY

At present, having received
no new offers or threatening directives,
one settles in for the tiresome work
of maintaining. The peaks and valleys
long stretching out before you
have all but vanished,
in their stead appears a wet mirage,
slick as dread on the horizon.
Ordinary folk, with little sense
of afternoon delight, often mistake this flatline
for defeat, hurrying to create imagined
tragedies to nurse themselves upon,
small nuclear warheads detonate,
though not every landslide within earshot is yours.
It is not right to gnaw on your own bones
like an abandoned puppy locked in a carry-on crate,
coping need not leave lasting scars.
The world is always ending, civilizations and
first cities fall, clocktowers tumble, books burn,
those responsible coast by like it was nothing,
your single worry saves none while sacrificing you.
This feeling, previously named intangible,
surprising and unrehearsed, is a bounty,
you are living temporal abundance,
be grateful,
recover in your earned comfort.
These last rough years, all grit and painful memory,

were a testament, you have absorbed and
emitted torment to the great pleasure
of many, withstanding mistakes, shame and wounded repute,
the reward for all that panic is this repose.
A soft illusion is for thinking through. Deciding
yourself again, perhaps for the first time
without urgency. Don't worry,
a person cannot disappear or disappoint
inside a moment of respite, soak it up,
allow yourself to starfish in this timeline,
sink deep in the warm water while it's warm,
everything cools eventually,
feel easy with your own company,
you have gifted yourself freshly washed hair
air-drying flat against your back after years
of frantically discovering yourself blown into traffic.

RUBY SUSAN

The man who loves me best
stood atop my father's rusted scaffold
reaching beyond himself to paint my eave's trim
after accepting my confessed fear of heights
without any necessary demonstration of horror.
When was this? One day, feels like ages ago now.
Time runs cottony under these rough conditions.
The sun was singeing the polar barrens, extravagant
and bright, so hot at that early hour as to be found
unbelievable. We squinted and smiled over our coffee cups.
Even the shrews scurrying in the long grass beyond
our modest border delighted in the lukewarm reprieve,
the shock of ardour reaching the undergrowth.
Some wonderful, beautiful, fine morning.
Perhaps we've gone tropical, or soft in the head,
these July temperatures upon our northern faces
bring about a gush of pleasantries and unnerving respite,
neither puff of wind nor lingering overnight squall.
Just warm feelings quietly churning alongside the shore.
The weather agreeing to be on best behaviour so
as not to send my calm man fleeing back to town.
Only whale breath punctuated the stillness.
They now summer-feed just off our ragged point,
whoosh and waves wet-lapping upon the landwash.
From the graveyard parking lot anyone
can watch them cresting and curling,
heaving themselves at the surface,

and anyone does, the ongoing procession
of strange vehicles, all colours and designs, steady
slink upon the gravel to see the sight, slowing just before
our front door to have a wee gawk at my lanky fellow.
Mealtime is showtime. All preen and performance,
a pantomime with its jaws wide, full to overflowing with baitfish
deemed lesser-than by men meaning to catch them all,
herring and mackerel, loosely scaled kippers
and bony sleek tinkers, tuna's tiny cousins,
small-eyed and sinewy, large mouths
clasping quick and fast gap, grasping, gulping,
scrappy summer-school rooms teeming with post-rolled
capelin, long reprimanded by the matron, their piddling
placement at the bottom of our livery barrel goes
unrewarded still, though so deserving they are
of our handsome gratitude and humble accolades
for centuries holding this hungry outfit up.
The blackflies swarmed my gentle man's brow,
sweat scenting them to him, they pitched and bit
at his nearly exposed ankles where borrowed
coveralls, too short for his lean stature,
pulled away from his socks. It is all a stretch for me,
I thought, wanting him immediately down from
an avoidable high place, exposed and at risk of harm,
the urgent need to have him once again safe upon
the ground overtakes all superficial pleasures
in a fresh facade, the weathered eave,
having to outwait my fear of further loss,
may be waiting forever.
Images of disbelief collide with this easy

picture of partnership. Having something, or
someone, to lose brings everyone down to earth.
Later, we will marry in the belly of his town, our
engagement party becoming a wedding, my best friends
frantically pinning together a bouquet from market roses
while I paint my fingernails, perched atop a turquoise
chair in nude hosiery a bit nip around the middle,
the lace dress that hung from Nanny's closet,
much sought-after and visited as a child, once
discarded in disappointment under sad plastic
in my mind's eye, there rested in the scene, atop a curved
brass bathroom hook just out of view, where beyond it I see a
multitude of endings, a flurry of possible futures revealing themselves,
and if all this comes to naught, as even he who loves me best
is surprised I've an opinion on everything,
know that we made you out of hope and desire, our want
magnified by swelling tenderness, closed in under unusual living
quarters, when the world seemed most uncertain, shrinking
and a fright, we found sure-footedness in your being,
and for a moment, as the calendar disrupted herself, liquefying
from day to week to month, you grew strong and untroubled,
shifting beneath the weight of our love in the time of COVID,
sucking your thumb, a self-soother already, named for your living grammies,
tucked deep within the folds of such earned and desperate joy.

ACKNOWLEDGEMENTS

I would like to extend my sincere thanks to Sarah MacLachlan, whose confidence in my artistic ability lends me the courage to brazenly pitch my unspoken aspirations in bagel shops and breweries across the land.

I would also like to thank my editor Damian Rogers as well as house poetry editor Kevin Connolly and managing editor Maria Golikova. Much gratitude to the extended team at Anansi for their patience and generosity bringing this book to fruition. Thank you to Michael Pittman, whose breathtaking work appears on the cover.

Many thanks to Sina Queyras and my Ph.D. committee and cohort at Concordia for their insights and feedback on my creative and academic work. My tireless agent, Samantha Haywood, continues to entertain my hot condemnations of inequity over the phone, and for this I am ever appreciative.

Always to my sisters, Melissa, Chelsie and Alicia, who accompany me through the ever-shifting landscape of my private and professional life. To my mom and dad, who continue to forge through all measures of time with admiral determination, passion and grit galore. And to my new extended family, the Pynes, who have welcomed me into their lives.

This collection is brimful to bursting with Nan and Pop Dredge, who cared for me at the start and continue to care for me still. It also holds much grief and gratitude for my Nanny and Poppy Coles as well as our relations and community members who were prematurely taken from us. I carry your memories into every fray and fight for the future we were meant to share. A special thank you to my big Newfoundland family: aunts, uncles and cousins.

A hearty shout out to my wild and accomplished friends across this country we now call Canada and especially those rooted on this island, also called Ktaqmkuk, where they choose to make their homes and careers alongside mine. Your steady presence and welcome encouragement bolster and inspire me.

And to Andrew, whom I love more than ink pressed into the paper page could ever communicate.

I wrote this for the young ones. Especially my nephews and my daughter. All deserving of a just, kind and thriving Newfoundland and Labrador.

Canada Council for the Arts, ArtsNL and the City of St. John's financially supported the writing of this collection. Thank you for the occasion of stability, which is never taken for granted.

Author photograph: Terry Day

MEGAN GAIL COLES is a graduate of Memorial University of Newfoundland and Labrador, the National Theatre School of Canada, and the University of British Columbia. She is the Co-founder and Artistic Director of Poverty Cove Theatre Company, for whom she has written numerous award-winning plays. Her debut short fiction collection, *Eating Habits of the Chronically Lonesome,* won the BMO Winterset Award and the Margaret and John Savage First Book Award, and it earned her the Writers' Trust of Canada 5×5 Prize. Her debut novel, *Small Game Hunting at the Local Coward Gun Club,* was a finalist for the Scotiabank Giller Prize and a contender for CBC Canada Reads, and it recently won the BMO Winterset Award. Originally from Savage Cove on the Great Northern Peninsula of the island of Newfoundland/Ktaqmkuk, Megan currently lives in St. John's, Newfoundland and Labrador, where she is the Executive Director of *Riddle Fence* and a Ph.D. candidate at Concordia University.